REDEMPTION!

New England's Fifth NFL Championship

TELEGRAM&GAZETTE

A GateHouse Media property

Paul Provost, publisher
Karen Webber, executive editor
David Nordman, assistant managing editor / sports
Camille Stinton, advertising director
Michele Marquis, consumer marketing director
Suzanne DeGeorge, marketing director
Anthony J. Simollardes, editor, editorial pages
Gary Hutner, Coulter Press publisher
Christine Ortoleva, finance director

Katherine Grigsby, Layout & Design

ISBN: 978-1-940056-50-0 (HC)
ISBN: 978-1-940056-51-7 (PB)

Printed in the United States of America
KCI Sports Publishing   3340 Whiting Avenue, Suite 5   Stevens Point, WI 54481
Phone: 1-800-697-3756   Fax: 715-344-2668
www.kcisports.com

CONTENTS

New England players celebrate after running back James White scored the game-winning touchdown in overtime to win Super Bowl LI. AP Photo

NEW ENGLAND PATRIOTS–NFL CHAMPIONS

The New England Patriots' road to a fifth Super Bowl title didn't begin with their 33-21 win over the Arizona Cardinals on Sept. 11.

It didn't begin on the first day of training camp either.

It began two weeks earlier, on July 15, when Tom Brady, the team's sure-bet Hall of Fame quarterback, announced he would accept a four-game suspension for his role in Deflategate.

"Say it ain't so?" Patriots fans asked.

Did Brady help under-inflate footballs before New England's 45-7 rout of the Indianapolis Colts in the 2014 AFC Championship?

We will never know, but he said he didn't. Coach Bill Belichick said he didn't and owner Robert Kraft said he didn't. And Patriots fans believed them.

They still do.

Fans stood by Brady during his 18-month standoff with NFL commissioner Roger Goodell. And they stood by him when he decided to give up his legal fight.

After all, they knew the only fight that mattered – the one played between the lines from September to February – had not yet begun.

This book chronicles that historic journey of redemption.

With Jimmy Garoppolo and Jacoby Brissett under center, and Brady far from Foxboro, New England started the season, 3-1. You couldn't have asked for better.

When Brady returned from exile to face the Cleveland Browns on Oct. 9 he was better than ever, throwing for more than 400 yards and three touchdowns in a 33-13 win.

Did Brady show any signs of rust?

Nope.

He was just warming up, we know now.

Brady led the Patriots to an 11-1 regular-season record, passing for 3,554 yards, 28 TDs and 2 interceptions – the best ratio in NFL history.

Of course, Brady will be the first to tell you that he had a great team around him – players and coaches – and he did.

LeGarrett Blount enjoyed the best season of his career, rushing for 1,161 yards and 18 touchdowns, while Julian Edelman caught 98 passes for 1,106 yards, and newcomer Martellus Bennett made up for the loss of Rob Gronkowski.

How about Chris Hogan, another off-season addition? His two TD catches helped the Patriots defeat the Pittsburgh Steelers in the AFC Championship.

And Dion Lewis, the undersized running back, who missed most of last year with a knee injury? All he did was score three TDs – one rushing, one receiving and one on a kick return – to beat the Houston Texans in the Divisional playoffs.

Up front, the team's offensive linemen almost never missed a snap in 2016. Shaq Mason, David Andrews, Marcus Cannon, Joe Thuney, Nate Solder all started at least 15 games. Now that's consistency.

The Patriots didn't lose on the road and their defense can take credit for that. Over the final seven games of the regular season, New England forced 14 turnovers, while holding their opponents to under 13 points per game.

AfterJamie Collins was traded, Malcom Butler, Logan Ryan, Patrick Chung, Devin McCourty, Dont'a Hightower, Trey Flowers and Rob Ninkovich kept the Patriots rolling.

All the way to a 34-28 overtime victory against the Atlanta Falcons in perhaps the greatest Super Bowl ever played.

Take that, Roger Goodell.

Redemption complete!

By Dave Nordman Assistant Managing Editor Sports

Head coach Bill Belichick raises a triumphant fist after receiving the Lombardi Trophy. AP Photo

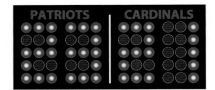

vs. Arizona Cardinals, Sept. 11, 2016
University of Phoenix Stadium
Phoenix, Arizona

GAROPPOLO SHINES IN DEBUT

By MARK DANIELS • *Providence Journal*

Jimmy Garoppolo did just what Tom Brady always seems to do. Lead the New England Patriots to a late score and victory.

But the Patriots needed a little help.

Arizona's Chandler Catanzaro missed a 47-yard field goal with 41 seconds to play and the severely depleted Patriots escaped with a 23-21 victory Sunday night in the season opener.

"We should have won the game," Cardinals coach Bruce Arians said. "As poorly as we played, we should have still won."

The snap from rookie long snapper Kameron Canady was low and holder Drew Butler didn't get the ball in terrific position. But Catanzaro was making no excuses.

"Just an old-fashioned miss," Catanzaro said. "I'll make the next one."

The miss came after Garoppolo, in his first NFL start, directed the Patriots from their own 19 to the Arizona 15 to set up Stephen Gostkowski's 23-yard field goal for what proved to be the winner with 3:44 to play.

Garoppolo completed 24 of 33 passes for 264 yards with no interceptions. He never seemed rattled.

"When you have confidence in your teammates

New England Patriots quarterback Jimmy Garoppolo (10) was 23-34 for 264 yards and 1 touchdown on the day. AP Photo

New England Patriots wide receiver Chris Hogan (15) pulls in a 37-yard touchdown pass to give New England a 7-0 first quarter lead. AP Photo

and they have confidence in you, it's easy to stay poised," he said.

Coach Bill Bilichick wasn't ready to crown Garoppolo the next Brady, though.

"He made some good plays. It is not perfect but he made a lot of good plays," Bilichick said.

Garoppolo was "a little amped up" to start the game as his first pass sailed over the head of Chris Hogan. He settled down and went on to complete four straight passes for 75 yards. He took advantage of blown coverage by Arizona rookie cornerback Brandon Williams on a throw to a wide open Hogan for 37 yards and a touchdown.

On their second possession, the Patriots drove from their 8 to the Arizona 29 and Gostkowski's 47-yard field goal made it 10-0.

Not only were the Patriots without Brady, suspended for his role in "deflategate," but they also didn't have tight end Rob Gronkowski, defensive end Rob Ninkovich and two starters on the offensive line.

Again, Garoppolo talked about that Patriot confidence.

"Whoever is out there we have confidence in one another," he said. "That is a good thing we have going for us."

A remarkable 45-yard run by David Johnson set up a 2-yard, sliding, over-the-shoulder touchdown catch by Fitzgerald that gave the Cardinals their only lead of the night, 21-20, with 9:46 remaining.

Ex-Patriot Chandler Jones sacked Garoppolo on the first play of New England's next possession, but the young quarterback still set up the winning kick by Gostkowski, who also booted a 53-yarder.

"I am really proud of our team tonight," Belichick said. "I thought we got great effort from all three phases. We played a good complimentary game."

New England, a five-point underdog, took the lead on its first possession and scored again to start the second half.

Up 10-7 at the break, the Patriots took the second-half kickoff and went 70 yards in nine plays. Williams was beaten badly for the second time on Garoppolo's 28-yard pass to the Arizona 8. LaGarrette Blount bulled it in from there and the Patriots led 17-7 with 10 minutes left in the first quarter.

The first two Arizona touchdowns followed New England turnovers.

New England Patriots running back LeGarrette Blount (29) pushes across the goal line for a third quarter touchdown as Cardinals free safety Tyrann Mathieu (32) and teammates defend. AP Photo

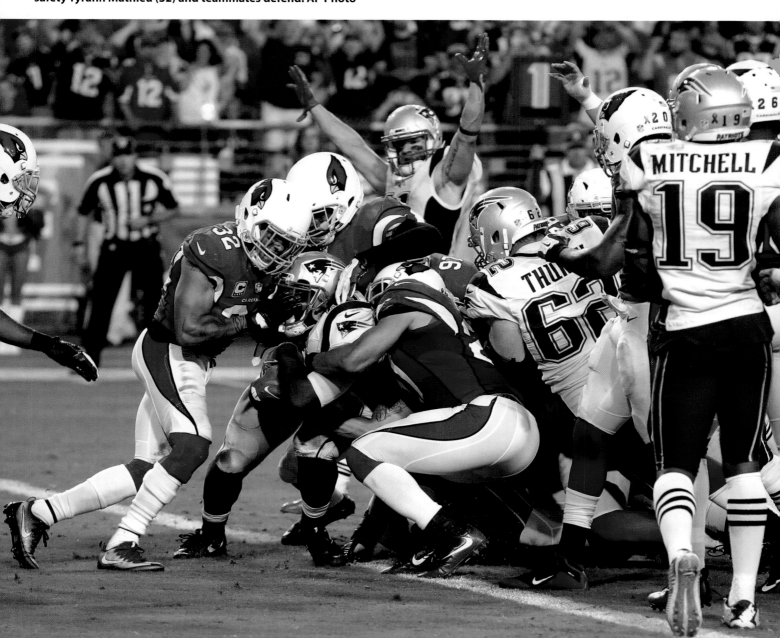

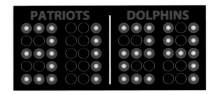

vs. Miami Dolphins, Sept. 18, 2016
Gillette Stadium
Foxboro, Massachusetts

PATS SURVIVE GAROPPOLO'S NIGHTMARE

By MARK DANIELS • *Providence Journal*

FOXBORO - It was Jimmy Garoppolo's worst nightmare.

Imagine having the game of your life; the performance you dreamed of as a kid. Then picture it being ripped away by the unforgiving football gods. The 24-year-old quarterback experienced all of that in the Patriots 31-24 win over the Miami Dolphins on Sunday.

In his first regular-season start in Gillette Stadium, Garoppolo made fans forget about Tom Brady for a moment. He also made prospective NFL teams and general managers drool over his potential. This was Garoppolo's moment, his time to shine and he did. He was electric, surgical and outstanding for a quarter and a half.

He was 18-for-27 for 234 yards and three touchdowns, a quarterback rating of 130.8 when it all came crashing down.

At 4:57 of the second quarter, Garoppolo showed why he's capable of not only being a starting NFL quarterback, but a good one. He used his athleticism to avoid the Dolphins pass rush and step out of the pocket. But as he released the ball, and connected with Malcolm Mitchell for 15 yards, he was hit after the throw by Kiko Alonso.

Garoppolo crashed down to the turf and landed

Patriots quarterback Jimmy Garoppolo receives attention from the team medical staff after landing hard on his right shoulder during first half action. AP Photo

on his right shoulder. As it turned out, that may be the last time we see the quarterback as a starter this season.

When the play was over, the quarterback immediately took a knee. He stood for a moment before dropping down again. That's when the Patriots training staff came out on the field. They were focused on Garoppolo's right shoulder and he was visibly in pain.

Garoppolo left for the locker room and never returned. Instead, the team immediately sent him to a local area hospital. The Providence Journal learned that as of Sunday night, it was believed that Garoppolo suffered a sprained AC joint in right shoulder. He'll miss Thursday's game against Houston and isn't guaranteed to be back in Week Four, but the possibility's there if he heals quickly.

"I turned around and see Jimmy on the ground. You hate to see that," Chris Hogan said. "He has worked so hard for this opportunity."

Losing a starting quarterback is the worst-case scenario for any team. On Sunday, with Brady out due to his four-game suspension, the Patriots were down to their third-string quarterback, rookie Jacoby Brissett.

For the next two games, Brissett (6/9 for 92 yards) could be the Patriots starter.

"[Garoppolo]'s a great guy," Brissett said. "And I hope he's well but when it's time to go, you just got to make sure you're ready to go."

The first few snaps for the third-round pick on Sunday were shaky but the Patriots were able to move the ball down the field later in the game. In a stadium that's generated plenty of story lines in the past, Sunday's injury to Garoppolo is the latest.

"Jimmy was playing unbelievable. The kid was playing lights out," Hogan said. "This is the NFL and that kind of stuff happens. We were fortunate enough that Jacoby was able to come in and step up."

To put the offensive performance by Garoppolo into perspective, the Dolphins defense came into this matchup after allowing just 12 points to Seattle a week ago. But it was evident from the first series, that Garoppolo was on his game.

The quarterback was perfect - 5-for-5 for 64 yards and a touchdown - in the opening drive, carving through the Dolphins' secondary. He capped the drive off with a 12-yard touchdown pass to Danny Amendola at 10:53 of the first quarter.

"Jimmy has all the capabilities in the world to be an amazing quarterback and he is. He was playing awesome today," Hogan said.

"He's a great player, puts a lot of work in. We'll hope for the best with his injury," Amendola added.

Facing Page: Patriots running back LeGarrette Blount (29) scores a 9-yard touchdown avoiding a tackle by Miami Dolphins rookie cornerback Xavien Howard (25) and safety Isa Abdul-Quddus (24). AP Photo

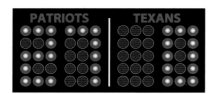

**vs. Houston Texans, Sept. 22, 2016
Gillette Stadium
Foxboro, Massachusetts**

MAKING TOAST OUT OF TEXANS

By MARK DANIELS • *Providence Journal*

Jacoby Brissett will never be confused for Tom Brady. He won't be mistaken for Jimmy Garoppolo, either.

As it turns out, that's not a bad thing.

If anything, Brady's four-game Deflategate suspension has given the Patriots a glimpse at their promising quarterback depth.

The Patriots entered the game against the Texans as an underdog; only the third time they weren't favored at home since 2002. Since they had to start their third-string rookie quarterback, it was understandable.

But as they've shown before, when the Patriots are counted out, they usually find a way to win. On Thursday, that meant climbing on the back of a young, inexperienced quarterback. And on this night, Brissett took his team for a ride, helping the Patriots to a 27-0 win over the Texans.

The Patriots offense didn't exactly look like the Patriots offense, but with Brissett, a change in tempo and emphasis on the run game was expected. What wasn't, was how elusive and effective Brissett was when running with the ball.

In his first NFL start, Brissett went 11-for-19 for 103 yards and rushed for 48 yards, including one dazzling touchdown run.

The rookie received a boost from the defense

Patriots quarterback Jacoby Brissett (7) dives into the end zone for a touchdown past Houston Texans linebacker Max Bullough (53) for a 10-0 New England lead. AP Photo

Patriots running back LeGarrette Blount (29) runs away from Houston Texans linebacker John Simon (51) and cornerback Kareem Jackson (25) on his way to a 41-yard touchdown in the fourth quarter. AP Photo

and special teams as the Patriots played a great game of complementary football to win with a rookie starting quarterback for the first time since the 1993 with Drew Bledsoe. LeGarrette Blount rushed for 105 yards and two touchdowns.

The Patriots jumped out to an early 3-0 lead, thanks to Stephen Gostkowski, but it didn't take long to see Brissett's rare blend of size (6-foot-4, 235 pounds) and athleticism.

On first down, at midfield, the Patriots ran a successful read-option play. As soon as the ball was snapped, Brissett faked the toss to Julian Edelman on his left and began to run. He then faked the toss to Brandon Bolden on his right, but instead kept the ball and faked out Whitney Mercilus before running and sliding for a gain of 13.

A 27-yard pass to Malcolm Mitchell set up Gostkowski's 24-yard field goal at 12:53 of the first quarter.

On the ensuing kickoff, Bolden stripped Houston returner Charles James and Duron Harmon recovered, giving the Patriots the ball. Two plays later, Brissett had his first NFL touchdown and wowed everyone in attendance.

The quarterback faked the handoff to Blount and executed a perfect bootleg run down the right sideline. Brissett ran 27 yards and shook off a tackle from safety Andre Hal en route to the end zone and the Patriots had a 10-0 lead. That was the longest touchdown run by a Patriots quarterback since Steve Grogan in 1976 (41 yards).

The offense stalled after that, but the defense stepped up and did all it could to help out the first-year quarterback. After the touchdown run, Jamie Collins intercepted Brock Osweiler for his second interception in as many games.

The first half ended with both offenses laboring, but the Patriots went into halftime with a 10-0 lead. In his first half as a starter, Brissett (59 passing and 41 rushing) accounted for 100 of the Patriots' 135 total yards.

Brissett & Co. extended the lead to 13-0 early in the third quarter.

Brissett's first pass of the second half went to Edelman for 23 yards. The Patriots then went run heavy, rushing the ball on eight of the next nine plays to get to the 10-yard line.

On third down, Brissett did a good job of avoiding the pass rush from J.J. Watt, but Edelman couldn't hang on to the pass and Gostkowski hit his second field goal.

Once again, on the ensuing kickoff, the special teams recovered a fumble. Nate Ebner forced Tyler Ervin to fumble and Jordan Richards recovered.

That put the Patriots at their 21-yard line. Two pass interference penalties, in the end zone, later and Blount scored on a 1-yard run to increase the lead to 20-0 at 9:19 of the third.

With 11:08 left in the game, Blount sprang loose for a 41-yard touchdown run to give the Patriots a 27-0 lead.

As it turns out, no Brady, no Garoppolo, no problem.

Patriots kicker Stephen Gostkowski (3) watches his successful 25-yard third quarter field goal split the uprights. AP Photo

Members of the New England Patriots and the Miami Dolphins along with guest Boston Red Sox designated hitter David Ortiz watch the coin toss by referee Craig Wrolstad. AP Photo

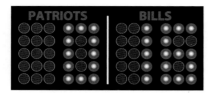

vs. Buffalo Bills, Oct. 2, 2016
Gillette Stadium
Foxboro, Massachusetts

FLAT PATS KO'D

By RICH GARVEN • *Telegram & Gazette*

FOXBORO - Tom Brady, Rob Ninkovich and Jimmy Garoppolo weren't the only Patriots absent for Week 4.

Their fellow NFL New Englanders failed to show up on offense, defense and special teams for varying - although, ultimately, debilitating - amounts of time as they were humbled by the brawling and bragging Buffalo Bills in a 16-0 setback Sunday at gloomy Gillette Stadium.

It was 60 excruciating and exasperating minutes of a lack of execution, leading to the previously perfect Patriots getting KO'd by an OK team that had lost 23 of the previous 25 meetings between these AFC East rivals.

"We think we're a better team than we showed today, but we just didn't do anything well enough today," a predictably grumpy Bill Belichick said of his 3-1 club, which saw its lead in the division reduced to a game as the Bills climbed to 2-2.

The Patriots hadn't played since Sept. 22, when they shut out the Houston Texans here. The story afterward was how all three phases collectively fed off one another to help carry rookie quarterback Jacoby Brissett to his first victory in his first professional start.

There was no complimentary football against the Bills, who became the first team to shut out the Patriots at home since Gillette Stadium opened in 2002.

Buffalo Bills linebacker Preston Brown, left, tackles scrambling Patriots quarterback Jacoby Brissett. AP Photo

Buffalo Bills safety Aaron Williams (23) breaks up a pass intended for Patriots wide receiver Chris Hogan, left, during the second half. AP Photo

The usually efficient and fundamentally sound Patriots did as much to hurt themselves as the boisterous Bills.

There were too many missed opportunities on offense and missed tackles on defense. Special teams contributed a missed field goal (Should we start worrying about Stephen Gostkowski?) and an absence of common sense by rookie kick returner Cyrus Jones, who got dressed in the locker room afterward with a towel draped over his head.

Rather than feed off one another to build momentum and a sense of teamwork, the Patriots' three units individually ate away at each other. In the process, they drained the life out of their sullen sideline one series at a time.

"I don't think each side was saying, 'What are we going to do now?'" safety Devin McCourty said. "But when you don't complement each other that's what you get."

The good news is the Patriots get the suspended duo of Brady and Ninkovich back beginning Monday after each player missed the first four games of the season.

The Patriots won three games without arguably the greatest quarterback in NFL history orchestrating the offense. They unleashed Garoppolo for six successful quarters before turning to Brissett to close out one win and squeeze out another.

But now Brady is back, ready to face a massive media contingent here this week looking for any sign of anger at Goodell and jealousy toward Garoppolo as he prepares to make what is expected to be a triumphant return next Sunday against the always hapless and still winless Browns in Cleveland.

"He's a good football player," receiver Danny Amendola said. "So we're excited to get Tom back. He's our leader."

That premature talk from the New England fan base of going 16-0 ended on a dreary day here, but - hey! - 15-1 isn't out of the question with Brady back at the helm and tight end Rob Gronkowski getting healthier by the week.

And there is still the possibility the offense will receive a boost from dynamic and diminutive running back Dion Lewis sometime in the coming weeks should his surgically repaired knee finally come around.

Patriots running back LeGarrette Blount (29) is upended by Buffalo Bills cornerback Ronald Darby (28). AP photo

COACH BILL BELICHICK

SIMPLY THE BEST

By MARK DANIELS • *Providence Journal*

FOXBORO - Bill Belichick doesn't need to flash his resume. Most know he's one of the greatest NFL coaches of all-time, but the longtime Patriots coach still surprises us from time-to-time.

Cases in point are these first three games of the 2016 NFL season.

In Week One, the Patriots were 9.5-point underdogs against the Arizona Cardinals before the upset win. That was the largest point spread against them since Super Bowl XXXVI when they upset the St. Louis Rams. To make it all the more impressive is that the win, on the road, came without Tom Brady.

That brings us to last weekend and Thursday night. After Jimmy Garoppolo goes down, the Patriots hold off the Miami Dolphins only to go into this last game with a rookie third-string quarterback. But as it turns out, this Patriots team is so well coached that Jacoby Brissett was able to help lead the team to its third straight win.

The Patriots beat the Houston Texans, 27-0, after entering the contest as 2.5-point underdogs at home. The start to the season even has Belichick's players impressed with their coach.

"In my opinion, he's the greatest coach to ever coach this game so anything he says, I'm going to do," said LeGarrette Blount, who rushed for 105 yards. "I feel like that goes for anyone on this team. The results speak for themselves."

The Patriots are now 3-0, without Brady, and have one more game, against Buffalo, before they get their future Hall of Fame quarterback back. But on Thursday, it was amazing to see how well the entire team executed.

Defensively, they not only held the Texans scoreless, but kept them out of the red zone. Houston wouldn't cross the 50-yard line until the final minute of the third quarter. Jabaal Sheard added two sacks and Jamie Collins (13 tackles) had an interception. On special teams, the kickoff unit forced two fumbles.

"Let me tell you man, Bill's game plan each week is the best game plan," Duron Harmon said. "He continues to amaze you with the things that come up in his mind to attack the offenses weakness."

Then there was Brissett. The rookie didn't make many mistakes and dazzled the crowd with his ability to run as the Patriots offense moved the ball up and down the field. With the win, Belichick tied Curly Lambeau with 226 regular season wins, tied fourth for the most all-time.

"Can't say enough about coach. It's been an honor to play here and work with him the last nine years," Matthew Slater said. "I've said several times that I think he's one of the best coaches not only in football, but all of pro sports. I think you saw that, along with his staff anytime you're on your third quarterback, it's not the best situation but Jacoby handled it great. The moment wasn't too big for him."

Patriots quarterback Tom Brady (12) confers with offensive coordinator Josh McDaniels and Coach Bill Belichick. AP Photo

Bill Belichick, left, watches his players along with his son, safeties coach Steve Belichick. AP Photo

Patriots quarterback Tom Brady threw for 406 yards and 3 touchdowns. AP Photo

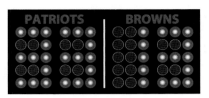

vs. Cleveland Browns, Oct. 9, 2016
First Energy Stadium
Cleveland, Ohio

BACK WITH A VENGEANCE

By KEVIN MCNAMARA • • *Providence Journal*

CLEVELAND - So Rob Gronkowski did you see any hesitation, any rust, in Tom Brady's repertoire in his ballyhooed return to the NFL Sunday?

"Did you? Me neither," Gronk answered with a smile.

How about you Chris Hogan? You've never played a game with Brady before and somehow, some way the two of you looked like old friends.

"He didn't look rusty to me," Hogan said. "I'm not surprised at all. I expect that and I think he expects me to make those kinds of plays."

Brady and the Patriots made all sorts of plays as order was officially restored around the NFL at FirstEnergy Stadium. With Brady's Deflategate nightmare over, the Pats dominated the hapless Cleveland Browns (0-5) from the opening gun and rolled, 33-13.

With their leader sidelined for the season's opening four games, the Pats juggled two injured quarterbacks yet somehow emerged with a 3-1 record. But now this team is no longer just holding things together. An offense that couldn't score a point only a week ago in a 16-0 loss to the Bills reached the end zone on each of its first three tries against the Browns and went on to roll up 24 first downs and 501 total yards.

Brady picked apart the Browns to the tune of 28-for-40 passing for a whopping 406 yards and three touchdowns. It was the eighth 400-yard passing game of his Hall of Fame career and for stretches

you could close your eyes and think Randy Moss and Wes Welker were still running routes. Brady spread the ball around to seven receivers, hitting Gronkowski over the middle, Hogan deep, Julian Edelman all over and the scary-talented Martellus Bennett (career-best three TD's) in the red zone.

"I tried to go out there and do the best I can do," Brady said. "That's what I try to do every week. It's what I always try to do. I know my teammates expect that of me, and that's what I expect out of them."

After what we saw transpire here, it's clear practice is vastly overrated. At least for the great ones like Brady.

Bill Belichick doesn't like hearing such blasphemy but what other conclusions can be drawn after seeing Brady slice-and-dice the Browns? In the last month, the QB was seen vacationing in Italy, hanging with friends at his alma mater (Michigan) and shooting commercials at a Boston-area prep school. He wasn't allowed to set foot in Foxboro, talk to any coaches or even watch team-produced game film.

No biggee. Brady and the Pats seamlessly worked onto the same page in three practices this week and were certainly ready to throw a busy playbook at the Browns.

"Tom Brady is one of the best players in this league that's probably ever played," said Browns' coach Hue Jackson. "Potentially he can go do that not just to us but he's done it to a lot of people before. We all know that. It's disappointing it happened but I'm not surprised by anything he does."

While Brady said he was happy to be back with his teammates and competing before thousands of Patriots fans, he deflected any and all Deflategate questions. As usual, his true feelings will stay locked in some memory bank back in Boston.

"This isn't the time for me to reflect," he said. "I'm just happy we won today. I have a job to do so there's no point in looking back at anything. None of it matters."

Patriots strong safety Patrick Chung (23) celebrates a second half interception with Devin McCourty, left, and Jonathan Jones (31). AP Photo

Patriots tight end Martellus Bennett celebrates one of his three touchdown catches against the Cleveland Browns. AP Photo

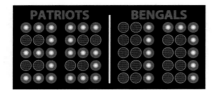

PATRIOTS | BENGALS

vs. Cincinnati Bengals, Oct. 16, 2016
Gillette Stadium
Foxboro, Massachusetts

BRADY ENJOYS HAPPY HOMECOMING

By MARK DANIELS • *Providence Journal*

FOXBORO - Tom Brady's homecoming turned into a duet performance on Sunday.

Of course, the quarterback didn't mind sharing the stage. Certainly not with the way Rob Gronkowski played.

After steamrolling the Cleveland Browns last weekend, the Patriots got some pushback from the Cincinnati Bengals on Sunday but Brady wouldn't allow his first home game of the 2016 season to be spoiled.

Brady faced more adversity in this contest than he did last weekend, but turned on the jets to complete 29-of-35 passes for 376 yards and three touchdowns. A big reason for the offensive outburst was Gronkowski. The tight end finished with seven catches for a career-high 162 yards and a touchdown.

A second-half surge pushed the Patriots (5-1), 35-17, over the Bengals.

"He's only gotten better as he's gotten older and understood more about the game and what he needs to do to prepare himself," Brady said of Gronkowski. "He just makes so many great plays."

"It's cool that I got the career-high and everything, but most important to me is getting that win," Gronkowski said. "That was a great team win overall."

Patriots quarterback Tom Brady takes the snap and scans the field. Brady threw for 376 yards and 3 touchdowns in his home debut. AP Photo

The connection between the two is nearing historic levels.

Brady and Gronkowski have connected for 65 touchdowns, second most in NFL history for a quarterback and a tight end. It's the seventh most all-time in NFL history between a quarterback and any target.

After catching one pass for 11 yards in two games without Brady, Gronkowski has 12 catches for 271 yards in two games since Brady returned from his suspension. Brady, meanwhile, has thrown for 782 yards and six touchdowns in two games.

"We feed off of what he does. He's consistently making huge plays," LeGarrette Blount said of Gronkowski. "It gives us a lot of energy, along with Tom."

The Patriots needed that connection more than ever on Sunday. They struggled in the first half, often losing the battle in the trenches. Brady was pressured, hit or sacked at least once on the first five series of the game.

After Stephen Gostkowski put the Pats ahead with a 46-yard field goal in the first quarter, the Bengals responded by taking the lead on a 2-yard touchdown scamper by Andy Dalton.

The Pats regained the lead on a 15-yard TD reception by James White and went into halftime with a 10-7 advantage.

The lead didn't last long, however. Brandon LaFell, the ex-Patriot, gave the Bengals a 14-10 lead at 11:19 of the third quarter.

After another Patriots drive ended following another sack, things turned around thanks to the defense. Linebacker Dont'a Hightower sacked Dalton in the end zone for his second safety in as many games as the Patriots inched closer, 14-12.

That play lit a fire under the offense as Brady and Gronkowski took over. Brady hit Gronkowski (38 yards) and Martellus Bennett (24 yards) for big gains on the ensuing drive. Brady capped it off by connecting with Gronkowski for a 4-yard touchdown, his first of the season.

On the next drive, Gronkowski's 38-yard reception set up another TD reception for White, which give the Patriots a 25-14 lead.

Following a Mike Nugent 25-yard field goal at 12:37 of the fourth, the Patriots responded with another Gostkowski field goal, this one from 31 yards. A Gronkowski 29-yard reception highlighted that drive.

"I mean, he's like a Clydesdale horse out there," Julian Edelman said. "It's fun to watch. Glad he's on our team."

Blount added a 1-yard touchdown with 57 seconds left to put the game out of reach.

"Brady! Brady! Brady!" chants broke out several times throughout the game.

"We feel it every time we take the field,' Brady said. "This is my home now; this is where my family lives. It's a great place. I love being here and I love being quarterback of this team. Hopefully I can do it for a long time."

With Gronkowski by his side, the possibilities are endless.

Patriots tight end Rob Gronkowski (87) stiff-arms the Bengals' Josh Shaw (26) on his way to the end zone during the third quarter. AP Photo

Patriots running back James White (28) scores on a 4-yard touchdown pass during the third quarter. White had two touchdowns on the day. AP Photo

Patriots running back LeGarrette Blount (29) gets past Pittsburgh Steelers inside linebacker Vince Williams (98) for a 5-yard touchdown run. AP Photo

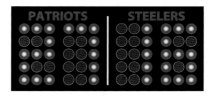

vs. Pittsburgh Steelers, Oct. 23, 2016
Heinz Field
Pittsburgh, Pennsylvania

BLOUNT CARRIES THE LOAD IN VICTORY

By MARK DANIELS • *Providence Journal*

PITTSBURGH -LeGarrette Blount's tenure with the Pittsburgh Steelers didn't end on a positive note as the back walked off the sideline during a Monday night contest against the Tennessee Titans after not receiving a single handoff. The team released him 24 hours later and Blount signed with the Patriots, where he's been a model citizen.

On Sunday night, against the team that let him go, Blount got his revenge in a performance that his Patriots teammates desperately needed.

Back in 2014, Blount ran for 266 yards and two rushing touchdowns in 11 games with Pittsburgh. He showed the Steelers brass he was more than capable of carrying the load on Sunday. Blount ran for a season-high 127 yards and scored two touchdowns to help push the Patriots over the Steelers, 27-16. The Patriots improve to 6-1 and hold a two-game lead over Buffalo in the AFC East.

This was the third time Blount went over 100 yards rushing this season. His two scores gave him a career-high eight touchdowns on the season.

"I'm having a blast. I've always loved it here," Blount said. "I have a great coaching staff, great teammates. It's really family oriented. We're always

Patriots tight end Rob Gronkowski (87) beats Pittsburgh Steelers strong safety Robert Golden (21) for a 36-yard touchdown during the second half. AP Photo

going to do whatever we have to do to get the job done."

On Sunday, that meant serving Blount the rock and his contributions were huge as the Patriots bumbled their way through the first half.

On the Patriots first series, Chris Hogan fumbled, giving Pittsburgh the ball back. Five play later, however, Malcolm Butler intercepted Landry Jones in the end zone. Tom Brady and the offense made amends on the ensuing drive and the Pats had a 7-0 lead, thanks to a 19-yard touchdown reception by James White at 3:03 of the first quarter.

It was clear in that first drive that the team would rely on Blount, who carried the ball six times in the opening series. It was also clear that the Steelers fans didn't forget about the back's exit. His first carry on Sunday garnered plenty of boos. The jeers didn't affect his performance.

"I just wanted to win a game just like I want to win every game," Blount said.

The Pats looked dominant on their second drive thanks to Blount, who had 50 rushing yards by the time he ran for a 3-yard touchdown to extend the lead to 14-0 at 11:01 of the second quarter.

But even with their backup quarterback, Landry Jones, the Steelers wouldn't go away quietly and they cut the lead in half, 14-7, with 9:02 left in the first half. Jones hit Darius Heyward-Bey for a 14-yard touchdown pass.

The miscues started to pile up after that. Two offensive drives ended with two drops on third down for the Patriots at the end of the second quarter. Steelers kicker Chris Boswell hit two of three field goals to bring the Pats lead down to 14-13.

Brady & Co. finally got back on the scoreboard at 6:27 of the third quarter to extend their lead to 20-13. Blount started the drive with runs of 11 and 25 yards. On third down, Brady hit Rob Gronkowski for a 36-yard touchdown.

The Steelers got another field goal and the Patriots clung on to a 20-16 lead with 14:49 left in the game.

The offense turned to Blount again on the next series as the back went over the 100-yard mark with an 11-yard gain. After a 37-yard reception by Gronkowski put the Pats at the 5-yard line, Blount tore through the defensive line again for his second touchdown to give the Patriots a 27-16 lead with 11:44 remaining.

"He gave us some explosive plays," Bill Belichick added. "We needed that particularly when they cut it to a four-point game."

After the score, Blount paused in the end zone and took a pretend selfie to celebrate, copying Steelers running back and friend Le'Veon Bell's celebration. Steelers fans were still booing, but it was clear the running back was in a much better place.

Thanks to his efforts, so were the Patriots.

Patriots cornerback Malcolm Butler (21) intercepts a pass in the end zone intended for Pittsburgh Steelers wide receiver Antonio Brown (84) during first half action. AP Photo

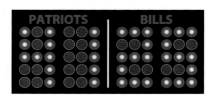

vs. Buffalo New York, Oct. 16, 2016
New Era Field
Orchard Park, New York

BRADY SHREDS BUFFALO IN WIN

By MARK DANIELS • *Providence Journal*

ORCHARD PARK, N.Y. - Despite getting pushed around in a Week 4 loss to Buffalo, the Patriots refused to get in a war of words in the week preceding Sunday's rematch.

They wouldn't talk about retribution or motivation after getting shut out at Gillette Stadium, where Jacoby Brissett got shoved by Bills safety Robert Blanton during warm-ups, igniting a small scuffle.

As it turns out, the Patriots didn't need to say a word.

With Tom Brady back, the only ones getting pushed around on Sunday were members of the Bills' defense. The Patriots quarterback again was outstanding, leading the Patriots to a 41-25 win over Buffalo.

"It's just great to come in here and put up all those points," Rob Gronkowski said. "(Buffalo) got that win, 16-0 (a few weeks ago). I'm so glad we came in here and showed them what we're really about."

Brady went 22 of 33 for 315 yards and four touchdowns. The 39-year-old now has 12 passing

Patriots quarterback Tom Brady (12) delivers one of his four touchdown passes on the day. AP Photo

Patriots wide receiver Julian Edelman (11) reaches for the goal line as he scores on a 12-yard touchdown pass and run good for a 31-10 third quarter lead. AP Photo

touchdowns in four games since returning from his Deflategate suspension. The Patriots improved to 7-1 and have a commanding lead over the Bills (4-4) and the rest of the AFC East as they head into their bye week.

Though he missed the first four games of the season, it's not crazy to think that Brady could be in the running for MVP.

Entering Sunday's game, all of Brady's touchdowns went to either tight ends or running backs. Against the Bills, that changed as three of Brady's four scores went to wide receivers in Julian Edelman, Chris Hogan and Danny Amendola.

"I've seen it for years. The guy's a tough SOB. It's a pleasure to get to play with a guy like him," Edelman said. "He's tough. You know, he's not the best for no reason."

Brady got to work right after the Bills opened the game with a 23-yard field goal from Dan Carpenter. Brady went 7-for-9 for 54 yards on the first drive, converting four third downs. The last conversion went to Amendola for a 9-yard touchdown with 4:35 left in the quarter.

"That was a big kind of start for us," Brady said. "We marched right down after that and scored a touchdown."

Hogan extended the Patriots lead to 14-3. Brady hit the wideout for a 53-yard touchdown as Hogan beat Stephon Gilmore with 1:41 left in the quarter. Two plays before the score, Brady took a big hit from Bills defensive end Jerry Hughes. His ability to bounce back is something that his teammates rallied around.

After Bills running back Mike Gillislee scored a touchdown, the Patriots responded again as Gronkowski set a Patriots record while extending their lead to 21-10.

Gronkowski hauled in a 53-yard touchdown with 4:18 left in the first half. The score was Gronkowski's 69th career touchdown, passing Stanley Morgan for the most TDs in Patriots history. The tight end took a bow before spiking the ball.

"I kind of had a feeling," Gronkowski said. "Just had to get up on the safeties' toes, give them a little move and cross the space. Tom read it super well and a great, great throw."

Amendola opened up the second half with a 73-yard kickoff return that put the ball on the Bills' 24-yard line. Two plays later, Brady hit Edelman for a 12-yard touchdown.

The Bills scored on the ensuing drive as quarterback Tyrod Taylor ran 26 yards into the end zone.

The Patriots fought back on the next drive as LeGarrette Blount put New England up, 38-17, with a 1-yard touchdown run.

Leading up to this game, several members of the Bills secondary talked about the Week 4 dust-up and how they wouldn't hesitate to push or fight any Patriots that got in their way during warm-ups once again.

There was no fighting before the game but when the whistle blew, the Patriots landed shot after shot.

By the time the clock hit zero, most of the Bills fans were already in the parking lot.

"I think the best part is the end," Brady said. "We have a lot of experiences where there are 70,000 people against you and at the end, there are 5,000 Patriots fans [in the stands cheering] on the road. That's a great motivation to us."

Patriots wide receiver Chris Hogan (15) runs away from the Buffalo Bills' Stephon Gilmore (24) for a 53-yard touchdown reception during the first half. AP Photo

BRADY TAKES HIGH ROAD ON DEFLATEGATE

By MARK DANIELS • *Providence Journal*

FOXBORO - The question was a bit leading, but it was a softball served right down the middle of the plate for Tom Brady. Ever since the Patriots booked a trip to Houston for Super Bowl LI, the Patriots quarterback has taken the high road when it comes to questions about Deflategate and NFL commissioner Roger Goodell.

On Friday, Brady was reminded of everything that transpired over the last two years. He was suspended. People called him a cheater. People lied. His name was tarnished.

"Are you telling us none of that factors into any of the motivation that you have to go out there and win this game so you can grab the trophy, hold it high, stand at the top of the mountain and howl at the moon?"

Brady paused and stared at the floor for a brief moment. Wearing a red Patriots winter hat, he smiled slightly and shook his head.

"I mean, I'm motivated for my teammates. I said that after the [AFC Championship] Game. I think that they're all the motivation that I need," Brady said. "And it takes a lot of work to get to this point, and nothing that's happened in the past is going to help us win this game. What's going to help us win this game is going through that process that we talked about and being ready to go. That's enough motivation for me."

You can debate Brady's source of motivation, but over the years, the future Hall-of-Famer made it a habit to prove people wrong. Being overlooked is part of Brady's story. What's made this tale great is how he has taken all that fuel and harnessed it into a career that's spanned 17 seasons.

Ask people who knew him at Junipero Serra High School in San Mateo, Calif., and they'll remind you how Brady worked hours on end doing the same footwork drills because he was told he wasn't good enough. Ask his friends and they'll tell you about his days at Michigan and how having to split time with Drew Henson only made him work harder in practice.

Tom Brady responds to a reporter's question during a recent interview. AP Photo

Watch the documentary, "The Brady Six," and you'll see this man cry when he remembers how he felt when he fell to the sixth round in the 2000 NFL Draft.

Without his fire or passion, Tom Brady wouldn't be Tom Brady.

The truth is, Brady was angry at the prospect of being called a cheater and having to sit out four games at the start of this season, but he isn't the type of person who would want his teammates or media to see that. Instead, he worked hard and pushed all his teammates to be better.

"In the locker room, he's always a positive guy. He's always trying to get guys going," Devin McCourty said. "You don't really see Tom come in and have a bad day. He's always ready to go, prepared. I think that professionalism rubs off on everybody else around him. All the things he has to go through, all the things he has to do to be the starting quarterback, to be Tom Brady, it would be easy to get frustrated at times, but he's always ready to go. Everybody in the locker room, no matter if you play offense, defense, you're a core special-teams guy, you can see how to be a great player, how to be ready to work every day if you just watch him."

Despite missing the first four games, Brady still threw for 3,554 yards and 28 touchdowns this season and at 39 years old still looked like the best quarterback on the planet. The questions about Goodell and Deflategate will remain, but Brady will remain on the high road all the way to his seventh Super Bowl.

"Well, I'm a positive person. So I just focus on all the positives, and I don't get caught up in negativity and bashing other people," Brady said. "I'm just very blessed. I get to do something I love to do - show up to work every day, play football in the National Football League, play for the Patriots. I grew up watching Joe Montana and Steve Young in the Bay Area at a great time. I've got great support from my family and some great support from my friends, and I love playing for this team.

"So I'm very blessed, and I try to keep a positive outlook and I try to influence people in a positive way. I try to be an encouraging person in other people's lives, and hopefully, that wears off on my teammates. It's a tough game. There's a lot of challenges that you face. And I think always focusing on what's positive has worked for me."

Displaying the work ethic during practices that keeps him at an elite level. AP Photo

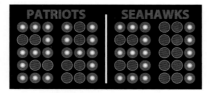

vs. Seattle Seahawks, Nov. 13, 2016
Gillette Stadium
Foxboro, Massachusetts

SEAHAWKS WIN THE SEQUEL

By RICH GARVEN • *Telegram & Gazette*

FOXBORO - The rematch was just like the original with the outcome hanging in the balance a yard from the goal line and just seconds remaining in a great game stuffed with memorable moments.

Unlike Super Bowl XLIX, the roles were reversed Sunday night at Gillette Stadium. This time it was the Patriots who had the ball and needed to reach the end zone.

And when they failed to score thanks to a terrific goal-line stand, the Seahawks headed back to Seattle with a 31-24 victory in tow.

"When you get a chance to (make a play) on the 1-yard line, nothing like it in football," Seahawks coach Pete Carroll said afterward. "It's one of the great challenges that a team and a defense gets."

It looked for sure like quarterback Tom Brady was going to complete the 38th fourth-quarter comeback of his Canton-bound career when the Patriots got a first down at the Seattle 2 with 43 seconds to go. But the Patriots were stymied by themselves and the Seahawks over the next four plays, the drive stalling 36 inches from the end zone.

"We've just got to do a little better job in that situation," coach Bill Belichick said. "I mean that's obvious."

Brady snuck his way for a yard on first down

Patriots tight end Rob Gronkowski (87) can't come up with a catch against the defense of Seattle Seahawks safety Cam Chancellor (31) on the game's final play. AP Photo

as the Patriots went heavy with a three-tight end set and fullback James Develin lined up in front of burly back LeGarrette Blount.

What's interesting is Brady and Belichick both admitted afterward scoring was only part of the equation. Clock management was also a factor, ostensibly because the Patriots didn't trust their defense.

"We were trying to get it very close but not in," Brady said.

"We were definitely trying to score but I'd say managing the clock was part of it," Belichick said.

The Patriots also went heavy on second down, which saw an air-bound Blount stopped for no gain by Seahawks safety Kam Chancellor. It was his 21st and final carry of the game, six of which went for zero or negative yards.

At this point the Patriots altered their approach a bit, spreading tight ends Rob Gronkowski and Martellus Bennett and receiver Julian Edelman wide with Blount lined up alone in the backfield.

"We have spread formations, we have tight formations, we have two backs in the backfield, one back in the backfield, no backs in the backfield," Belichick said. "I mean whatever we do on any of those is to try to create some type of advantage in some way for the play that we have."

The plan was for Brady to attempt a sneak behind a six-man line, but it was aborted with a botched snap that put the ball back at the 2. Brady said it was a miscommunication error on his part as center David Andrews thought he was going straight instead of left.

It was the third straight play into the gut of a stout defense. Deciding whether to stick with something because of a belief it will work versus recognizing it's the football equivalent of pounding one's head into a wall is something every coaching staff deals with.

"You have to decide whether you want to just do it again and kind of get it right or do something else," Belichick said.

The Patriots decided it really isn't what they wanted, so on fourth down they opted for a fade pass to Gronkowski in the left corner of the end zone. But he got tangled up with Chancellor and when the officials opted to not call pass interference, the Patriots had lost for the second time in nine games this season.

"Sometimes you get the call, sometimes you don't," Brady said. "So, certainly, it looks like it came down to one play, but there were a lot of plays in this game that we could have done a better job of."

And if they had done just that on one of their final four offensive plays, the sequel would have turned out just like the original.

Patriots wide receiver Julian Edelman (11) hangs on to make a tough catch during the first half. AP Photo

Patriots running back LeGarrette Blount celebrates a touchdown run with the End Zone Militia. AP Photo

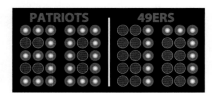

vs. San Francisco 49ers, Nov. 20, 2016
Levi's Stadium
Santa Clara, California

HAPPY HOMECOMING FOR BRADY

By MARK DANIELS • *Providence Journal*

SANTA CLARA, Calif. - Ominous clouds sat high above Levi's Stadium on Sunday. They signaled how many were feeling about this Patriots team coming off a tough loss to the Seattle Seahawks last weekend.

The Patriots came into this contest with the San Francisco 49ers with plenty of questions about a defense that struggled to get to the quarterback and stop big pass plays. The offense came into this game after being shutdown on the goal line last weekend.

It turns out that a 49ers team, having lost eight games in a row, was just what the doctor ordered.

The Patriots weren't perfect on Sunday, but they weren't going to let the heavy rain or the 49ers stop them in this 30-17 win. The Patriots improved to 8-2, getting a nice combined effort from the offense and defense.

Tom Brady led the way in his first start on the road against the team he grew up rooting four. The offense struggled for a brief moment in the middle of this game, but Brady led the way with four touchdown passes as the Pats turned on the jets in the fourth quarter.

Patriots wide receiver Malcolm Mitchell (19) scores on a 56-yard touchdown pass from Tom Brady. AP Photo

Julian Edelman (11) catches a 4-yard touchdown pass in the corner of the end zone for a 6-0 first quarter Patriots lead. AP Photo

In the first half, it was a mixed bag for the Patriots. There were moments were they looked dominant and times when they looked anything but.

The Pats had a 13-3 lead early in the contest. Brady hit Julian Edelman for a 4-yard score on their first series and then James White for a 9-yard touchdown on their second. The score between Brady and Edelman, two people from the area was special.

"That's something you kind of dream about," Edelman said. "Being from here, coming back and playing the Niners with Tom Brady, score a touchdown on the opening drive in a rain storm. It's cool."

The Patriots defense gave a Jekyll and Hyde performance in the first half. They allowed the 49ers to drive down to the 3-yard line on their second series, but a Dont'a Hightower sack forced San Franicsco to settle for a Phil Dawson field goal.

The Patriots only went into halftime, however, up 13-10 after Colin Kaepernick hit Vance McDonald for an 18-yard touchdown. On that drive, 49ers gashed the Patriots defense traveling 92 yards in 4:17.

All of a sudden, the Patriots offense couldn't score. After scoring touchdowns on the first two drives of the game, the offense punted/failed to score on the next five series. The team also had a 35-yard touchdown by Blount wiped out in the second quarter due to a hold. Both teams went scoreless in the third quarter - credit goes to the Patriots defense for cleaning up their play.

"We had good field position to start the game and two drives where we got it in," Brady said. "We had great field position and took advantage of it. We had some penalties that got us off track and they played some good defense."

The Patriots confidence never wavered and stuck to their original game plan. It wasn't easy without Rob Gronkowski or Chris Hogan, but the team stepped up in the fourth quarter getting two touchdowns and a field goal.

Brady hit Danny Amendola for a 6-yard score at 14:55 of the fourth quarter. On that drive, he had four pass plays of 13-plus yards to Malcolm Mitchell (21), White (14), Martellus Bennett (14) and Edelman (13).

Mitchell had the best day of his NFL career catching four for 98 yards and his first touchdown. Mitchell's 56-yard touchdown at 6:16 of the fourth quarter, extended the lead to 27-10. LeGarrette Blount also had another banner day, rushing for 124 yards on 15 carries.

"You're not going to put up points every play you make. It takes drive, it takes consistency," Blount said. "That's what we continue to do. We stay consistent. We stuck with the game plan. We drove the ball down the field and we got points."

Stephen Gostkowski extended the lead to 30-10 with a 38-yard field goal at 6:16 of the fourth quarter. Kaepernick hit Shaun Draughn for a 13-yard touchdown with 2:09 left, but it was too little too late for the 49ers.

San Francisco 49ers quarterback Colin Kaepernick (7) tries to escape from Patriots strong safety Patrick Chung (23) and defensive end Trey Flowers (98) before Chung sacked him during the first half. AP Photo

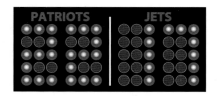

PATRIOTS | JETS

**vs. New York Jets, Nov. 27, 2016
MetLife Stadium
East Rutherford, New Jersey**

BRADY SPEARHEADS ANOTHER LATE COMEBACK

By MARK DANIELS • *Providence Journal*

EAST RUTHERFORD, N.J. - Fans at MetLife Stadium chanted his name throughout the game on Sunday, and Tom Brady needed all the help he could get.

After missing two practices last week with a knee injury, the Patriots quarterback moved around the field and away from defenders with a noticeable limp. No one said winning in the NFL was easy, and that was certainly the case on Sunday.

Brady was battered and already bruised, but nevertheless led his team back from another fourth-quarter deficit. This time, Brady's 50th career game-winning drive put him in the NFL history books.

The Patriots beat the Jets, 22-17, and with the victory, Brady tied Peyton Manning with the most wins in NFL history with 200.

"It was a great win for our team," Brady said. "We didn't play as well as we wanted to, but we made the plays when we needed to."

Down by one point, 17-16, Brady got the ball with 5:04 left in the game. As he's done 49 times before, he led the Patriots down the field with time fading away.

Brady hit Julian Edelman (24 yards) and Dion Lewis (16 yards) to get the Patriots past midfield at the

Patriots wide receiver Malcolm Mitchell (19) pulls in a 4-yard touchdown reception. AP Photo

Patriots defensive end Chris Long (95) gets a hand on the ball as New York Jets quarterback Ryan Fitzpatrick (14) throws, causing a fumble that was recovered by teammate Trey Flowers. AP Photo

43-yard line. After two incomplete passes, Brady went back to Edelman for a gain of six to set up a fourth-and-4.

With the game on the line, Brady hit James White at the line of scrimmage. The running back then beat Jets linebacker Darron Lee for the four yards the Patriots needed.

Chris Hogan was up next, and after the first down he caught a 25-yard pass, giving the Patriots a first-and-goal from the 8 with 2:00 remaining. Brady had a tough week, but his toughness motivated those around him.

"He's the leader of our offense," Hogan said of Brady. "Nothing's really going to keep him out of a game. When you see our leader coming out here like that, not 100 percent, you want to just play a little bit harder for him."

On the next play, Brady hit Malcolm Mitchell for the game-winning touchdown. It was the second score of the day for the rookie. A James White two-point conversion was no good, but the Patriots preserved their 22-17 lead for the win.

"At first I thought it was going to Julian, but then I realized he wasn't reaching for it, so I thought maybe I should," Mitchell said.

The Patriots improve to 9-2 and had to work extra hard for this one.

New England's first three drives had a common theme: they all ended with punts by Ryan Allen, and Brady was tortured. The quarterback was hit three times during the first three drives as the constant pressure put the Patriots in an early hole.

The Patriots didn't get going offensively until a trick play moved them downfield.

At 10:46, Brady threw a pass to Hogan behind the line of scrimmage. The receiver then threw a deep ball to Mitchell. The pass from Hogan was incomplete, but a pass interference call set up a Stephen Gostkowski 28-yard field goal at 10:48 of the second quarter.

A Malcolm Butler forced fumble and fumble recovery at 9:46 of the second led to Mitchell's first touchdown, a 4-yard score at 6:34 of the second quarter. The Pats took a 13-10 lead, thanks to a Gostkowski field goal at 7:37 of the third.

With 10:17 left in the game, Fitzpatrick hit Quincy Enunwa for a 22-yard leaping touchdown catch. Though the play was first ruled incomplete, the officials reversed the call and the Jets held a 17-13 lead.

Mitchell wasn't able to corral a touchdown pass, but Gostkowski hit a 41-yard field goal to bring the Jets' lead down to 17-16 with 7:02 remaining. After a defensive stop, Brady went back to work and back to Mitchell. After the rookie's game-winning touchdown, Chris Long strip-sacked Fitzpatrick and Trey Flowers recovered.

"We played our best football when it counted the most," Belichick said. "That's always important."

"I've had a lot of great support over the years," Brady said when asked about win No. 200. "Hopefully, we keep winning. It never gets old."

With the win over the Jets, Patriots quarterback Tom Brady (12) tied Peyton Manning for the most wins in NFL history with 200. AP Photo

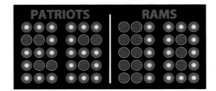

vs. Los Angeles Rams, Dec. 4, 2016
Gillette Stadium
Foxboro, Massachusetts

DEFENSE DOMINATES RAMS

By RICH GARVEN • *Telegram & Gazette*

FOXBORO - It was the kind of defensive effort that was expected of the Patriots on a weekly basis entering the season, but was rarely seen over the first three months.

That would be stout and stingy, dependable and dominate.

The Patriots gave up too many yards and produced too few turnovers in the first 11 games. They were unable to consistently generate a pass rush and made mediocre quarterbacks like Tyrod Taylor, Landry Jones and Ryan Fitzpatrick look marvelous.

But the mantra around Gillette Stadium last week was how it was December, which means it's time to play your best football of the year.

The defense took it to heart, clamping down and bottling up the Los Angeles Rams in a 26-10 victory at Gillette Stadium.

"We played well," cornerback Logan Ryan said. "We played about 59 minutes and obviously you want to finish better than that. But for most of the day we were locked in."

Los Angeles Rams wide receiver Brian Quick (83) is tackled by New England Patriots safety Patrick Chung (23) and linebacker Dont'a Hightower (54). AP Photo

Patriots cornerback Malcolm Butler (21) celebrates an interception with teammates Duron Harmon (30) and Eric Rowe (25). AP Photo

The Rams were held to 162 yards - including 25 in the first half - with 66 coming on a reception by receiver Kenny Britt. Two plays later, Britt caught a 1-yard touchdown pass with 75 seconds to play.

The Patriots allowed a season-low seven first downs, got off the field on third down 11 out of 12 times, allowed an average of 2.8 yards a rush, and best of all forced turnovers and regularly hurried, harassed and hit rookie quarterback Jared Goff.

The Patriots got their hands on nine of Goff's 32 passes with cornerback Malcolm Butler and linebacker Kyle Van Noy coming up with interceptions. Defensive end Jabaal Sheard had three passes defensed, matching his total in the previous 23 games, and came close to interceptions on two of them.

Tom Brady & Co. parlayed the takeaways into 10 points.

It was the Patriots second straight game with two takeaways after having one in the previous five outings.

"The coaches preach it all the time, 'Go for the ball,' " Sheard said. "That's part of defense, trying to turn the ball over. We did an OK job today, but there's always room for improvement."

Van Noy's interception was the first of his career and came on a pop-up after Sheard busted through a double team and hit Goff as he was throwing. That was one of nine hits on the QB, who was sacked four times.

Five players had at least a hit with linebacker Shea McClellin, cornerback Logan Ryan and defensive ends Rob Ninkovich and Chris Long collecting sacks. The Patriots have 13 sacks in their last four games, matching their total in the first eight games.

It was, they believed, only a matter of time until they went from hauling down passers to just getting a hand on them.

"There were weeks when people were like, 'Where's the pass rush?' and I think it was very close," Long said. "It was closer than people know and when you watch the film you can see that.

"But on a day like today we all just worked together really well and we were able to get there a lot. And it came from all over. It was a complete team win, a complete defensive win and we're proud of that. Now we'll have to build on it."

They'll look to build on it in their upcoming Monday night matchup here with the Baltimore Ravens.

Ideally producing another dominant December defensive effort, the kind rarely seen in September, October and November.

Patriots wide receiver Julian Edelman (11) makes an acrobatic catch in front of Los Angeles Rams safety Maurice Alexander (31). AP Photo

SURGING EDELMAN KEY FOR PATS

By RICH GARVEN • *Telegram & Gazette*

FOXBORO - The Patriots don't have a receiver who is as talented and productive as the Pittsburgh Steelers' Antonio Brown, which puts them in the same category as the vast majority of NFL teams.

Brown, a first- or second-team All-Pro selection each of the past four seasons, has a league-leading 481 receptions - or 83 more than anyone else - since 2013 due to a blend of speed, strength, stamina, quickness and competitiveness.

The Patriots, though, counter with a consistently excellent and occasionally great receiver of their own in Julian Edelman. The former Kent State quarterback has 356 receptions over the past four seasons, a total topped only by Brown, Demaryius Thomas (398), Julio Jones (364) and Larry Fitzgerald (361).

Edelman enters the AFC Championship Game on Sunday against the Steelers hotter than a habanero.

He caught eight of 13 targeted passes for 137 yards and five first downs in the divisional round victory over the Houston Texans. That occurred two weeks after he closed the regular season with eight catches for a career-high 151 yards, a TD, five first downs and a two-point conversion in a win over the Miami Dolphins.

Edelman is averaging 17.9 yards a catch in his last three games, well above his career average of 10.7. He's had 100-plus receiving yards in three of the past six games after surpassing the century mark nine times in the first 110 games of his career.

"I think that's just trying to improve each week," Edelman said of a second-half surge that has resulted in 65 receptions in the last nine games after making 41 in the first eight.

"Just trying to do what I'm told, and when opportunities are coming your way, you've got to take advantage of it. So, that's what I've been trying to do."

Edelman had a season-high nine receptions in the Patriots' 27-16 win over the Steelers in Pittsburgh in Week Seven. But he was limited to 60 yards and two first downs and lost a fumble on a punt return.

That setback happened during a four-game losing streak for the Steelers, who have since won nine straight and advanced to the AFC Championship Game for the first time since 2010. The surge has been bolstered by an improved defense that has allowed 16.5 points during the winning streak.

"It really looks like they've come into their own," Edelman said. "They're playing as a unit pretty darn well, probably the best we've seen this year. They're fast, they're athletic, they're young, but they also have veterans in key spots to help them know the game a little more."

Those youngsters include three rookies who start on defense, including two in the secondary in cornerback Artie Burns and strong safety Sean Davis.

The 6-foot, 197-pound Burns was drafted 25th overall out of Miami. He had a team-high three interceptions and 10 additional passes defensed in 16 regular-season games, the last four of which he

started, along with both playoff wins.

Davis, who was taken in the second round (58th overall) out of Maryland, also has good length and size at 6-1 and 201 pounds, and played in all 16 games. He finished fourth on the team in tackles with 54 and added 1.5 sacks and an interception.

"The kid's got it all; he's got the athleticism, the speed, length," Edelman said of Burns. "So, he's definitely been playing well. He's been playing more and that's for a reason. Davis, he's playing well, too. I'm more focused on cornerbacks, but you definitely have to take those guys into consideration as well."

Steelers coach Mike Tomlin believes his rookie defensive backs will be up to the challenge of trying to cover not only Edelman, but the likes of Danny Amendola, Michael Floyd, Chris Hogan, Malcolm Mitchell and, whew, Martellus Bennett.

It's almost imperative if the Steelers are to leave here with the Lamar Hunt Trophy and an invitation to Super Bowl LI.

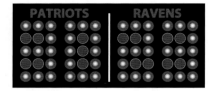

vs. Baltimore Ravens, Dec. 12, 2016
Gillette Stadium
Foxboro, Massachusetts

DEFENSE GETS FLACCO TO LOSE 'COOL'

By RICH GARVEN • *Telegram & Gazette*

FOXBORO - The Patriots were coming off their most dominant and decisive defensive effort of the season as they renewed their deliciously detestable rivalry with the Baltimore Ravens on Monday night at Gillette Stadium.

And the quarterback they were intent on containing and corralling in prime time was coming off his best passing performance in what has been another characteristically eventful and uneven season.

The NEP D versus a red-hot "Joe Cool" Flacco was a matchup of the utmost importance as the Patriots sought to take another step toward their inevitable clinching of the AFC East and the Ravens looked to move back into a first-place tie with the Pittsburgh Steelers in the AFC North.

Advantage: New England.

The defense made its presence felt from its first play until the waning moments of the fourth

---

Patriots defensive end Rob Ninkovich (50) sacks Baltimore Ravens quarterback Joe Flacco (5) during second half action. AP Photo

Patriots wide receiver Chris Hogan (15) catches a 79-yard touchdown pass in the fourth quarter. AP Photo

quarter as it co-starred in the Patriots' fourth straight victory, this one a 30-23 decision that raised their record to 11-2.

"It was a good performance for us," defensive end Chris Long said after the Patriots held the Ravens to three field goals and, following special teams turnovers, a pair of short-field touchdowns.

"We were resilient. We would have liked to shut the door on those two turnovers, but at the end of the day I think we did a good enough job to win."

Flacco is now 3-6 all-time against the Patriots. It was his seventh game at Gillette Stadium. He has two wins - both in the playoffs - with the five losses all coming by seven points or less.

Flacco, as has been the case throughout the season, didn't have the benefit of a run game and had no choice but to drop back, pass and repeat. That's generally not a recipe for success.

The ninth-year pro was 37 of 52 for 324 yards and two touchdown passes. He was intercepted once, sacked twice and had four passes tipped.

The run game, which came in ranked 28th in the league, produced 42 yards on 14 carries (3.0 average).

"That's always a plus, anytime we can get pass deflections or him just being aware of the rush and not being able to look down the field," Flowers said. "So we got a turnover out of him. We had him in check pretty well."

All told, the Ravens, who scored a season-high 38 points in a win over the Miami Dolphins the previous game, finished with 348 yards and 17 first downs as they were 6 of 16 (38 percent) on third down.

A muffed punt in the third quarter by rookie Cyrus Jones gave the Ravens the ball at the New England 3. Two plays later, Flacco found reserve tight end Darren Waller wide open in the end zone for a 3-yard TD toss that cut the deficit to 23-10 with 6:50 left in the quarter.

The ensuing kickoff was fumbled by veteran Matthew Slater at the New England 22. Flacco needed four plays and 79 seconds to capitalize, his 8-yard pass to running back Kenneth Dixon making it a six-point game.

"If you want to be a great defense you have to be great when there's a little bit of adversity and that's the next step," Long said. "Again, it was a team win. We did a great job in the first half and we need to clean up a few things in the second half, but we'll get there."

Patriots rookie wide receiver Malcolm Mitchell (19) celebrates his 6-yard touchdown reception. AP Photo

Denver Broncos quarterback Trevor Siemian (13) looks to pass as Patriots defensive lineman Trey Flowers applies pressure. AP Photo

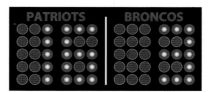

vs. Denver Broncos, Dec. 18, 2016
Mile High Stadium
Denver, Colorado

PATS CLINCH EIGHTH STRAIGHT AFC EAST TITLE

By MARK DANIELS • *Providence Journal*

DENVER - Heading into Sunday's matchup, there had been plenty of talk about the troubles Tom Brady and the Patriots offensive line have had against the talented Denver Broncos defense.

The Patriots defense apparently took notice.

On Sunday, Brady emerged from Denver as a winner for the first time since the 2011 season, but the Patriots' 16-3 victory over the Broncos had little to do with the quarterback. Instead, the triumph was all about a motivated Patriots defense.

"This was big for us," Patriots cornerback Logan Ryan said. "I've been here for four years and haven't won in Denver. How they ended our year last year, this was definitely a personal game for us. I don't care what anyone says - We wanted to come out here and completely dominate the game and make [Denver QB Trevor Siemian] look like a young quarterback."

With the win, the Patriots improve to 12-2, clinch the AFC East title and are guaranteed a first-round bye in the playoffs.

Brady (16 for 32 for 188 yards and no touchdowns) had his worst game of the 2016 season, showing the Broncos are still his kryptonite. But

Patriots running back LeGarrette Blount (29) sneaks across the goal line to score the only touchdown of the day. AP Photo

the quarterback got bailed out by a shutdown performance from the Patriots' top-10 defense.

Patriots' defenders got ample pressure on Siemian throughout the game and played well in the secondary to thwart any offensive momentum.

The first quarter was a forgettable one for Brady. In four drives, he went 0 for 6 - just the second time in his career that has happened - and the Patriots made only one first down.

After the Pats opening drive, Broncos returner Jordan Norwood muffed Ryan Allen's punt and rookie Jonathan Jones recovered the fumble. The Pats took over on the Denver 31 and Stephen Gostkowski eventually was able to hit a 45-yard field goal for 3-0 lead at 12:32 of the first quarter.

The Broncos tied the game at 7:02 of the quarter when Brandon McManus connected on a 33-yarder.

It looked like the Broncos were going add to their total but Ryan intercepted a Siemian pass just as the second quarter began. The turnover halted a Broncos' drive that had brought them to the 14-yard line.

"That was huge," Devin McCourty said. "That's the type of plays that win games, win big games down the stretch."

Brady finally woke up after that, completing his first pass of the day at 14:05 of the second quarter. At 11:01, LeGarrette Blount bulled his way into the end zone from two yards out and after Gostkowski's PAT, the Pats had a 10-3 lead. The touchdown was Blount's 15th of the season, breaking Curtis Martin's Patriots franchise record.

The Blount touchdown was the only time the Patriots would find the end zone in the game. The team relied heavily on Gostkowski, getting two field goals in the second half (from 40 and 21 yards) to extend the lead to 16-3.

That was plenty for the defense and it didn't allow a first down on Denver's first five drives of the second half. The Broncos had 19 total yards on their first 15 second-half plays. After getting a sack from Trey Flowers in the first half, the defense came up with three more - from Jabaal Sheard, Malcolm Brown and Flowers again - in the second half.

"It's a good time to play your best football for sure," Chris Long said. "You can kind of feel it building up. We'll just kind of continue to improve, keep trying to get turnovers, keep disrupting the quarterback."

The Broncos started to drive down the field late in the fourth, but McCourty came up big on fourth-and-2. The safety hit Demaryius Thomas, forcing the receiver to drop a potential first-down reception. McCourty then recovered a Norwood fumble on the final Broncos' play of the game.

"It was a great feeling. It was a great team win," said Brady, who won in Denver for only the third time in 10 games.

Patriots defensoive lineman Jabaal Sheard (93), Malcom Brown (90) and Trey Flowers (8) celebrate Brown's sack. AP Photo

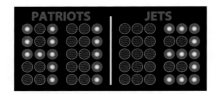

vs. New York Jets, Dec. 24, 2016
Gillette Stadium
Foxboro, Massachusetts

PATS ROLL JETS

By RICH GARVEN • *Telegram & Gazette*

FOXBORO - Tom Brady struggled his last time out, which wasn't surprising considering the defense-dominant Broncos were the opponent and the game was in Denver, an historic house of horrors for the GQ/QB.

Brady was looking to get back on track in what has been an NFL MVP-worthy season against the New York Jets on Saturday in a Christmas Eve matinee.

The still-hated, now-dreadful Jets have frequently given Brady fits over the years. Not this time.

Brady threw for 171 yards and three touchdowns in the first 30 minutes as the Patriots opened a 27-0 lead while on their way to a 41-3 victory in conditions that ranged from rainy to sunny at merry Gillette Stadium.

"It was a great win," Brady said after being the Jets for the 23rd time in his career, making him the first quarterback in league history to record at least 23 wins against two opponents, the other being the Buffalo Bills.

"We played in some tough conditions and displayed some mental toughness. So it was a great win - 13-2 is pretty good."

The Patriots extended their winning streak to six games and improved to 13-2. In the process, they positioned themselves to clinch the top seed in the AFC playoffs with a win in the regular-

Patriots tight end Matt Lengel, right, celebrates his first touchdown catch of the season with teammates Malcolm Mitchell, left, and Julian Edelman (11). AP Photo

Patriots defensive back Eric Rowe, left, intercepts a pass intended for New York Jets wide receiver Brandon Marshall (15) during the first half. AP Photo

season finale against the Dolphins in Miami or an Oakland loss at Denver.

Brady anticipates he'll make his 12th straight start.

"We've got eight days before we play Miami, but I expect to go out there and play my best," he said.

All told, Brady finished 17 of 27 for 214 yards and the aforementioned three TDs before giving way to backup Jimmy Garoppolo with less than a minute to play in the third quarter. He didn't throw an interception - meaning that's two picks in 399 attempts this season - and was sacked once as he generally received solid protection from his big blockers.

In the holiday spirit, Brady took care of all his receivers. Nine were targeted at least once, and eight made at least one reception, led by BFF WR Julian Edelman with five catches for 89 yards.

In the decisive first half, Brady excelled on the deep ball. He had touchdown passes of 18 yards to reserve tight end Matt Lengel and 25 yards to running back James White and picked up first downs via receivers Edelman (35 yards), Chris Hogan (18) and Malcolm Mitchell (16), and tight end Martellus Bennett (14), who also had a 5-yard TD catch.

In addition, Mitchell drew a 49-yard penalty via pass interference on a deep ball on the play prior to White's touchdown, which came with 25 seconds left in the first half.

"A lot of guys made plays today, so it was nice," Brady said. "Matt got his first touchdown pass, so that was pretty cool. I would say he really wasn't the first option on the play, but he sprung free, and it ended up being a big play in the game.

"Between guys like that and the usual suspects, we made some plays down the field. I thought the ones before halftime were pretty big because they gave us some momentum going into the second half. There was the PI, and then the play to James."

The passing game stagnated in the third quarter, and Brady fumbled after being sacked by defensive lineman Sheldon Richardson with about four minutes gone. But Brady somehow extended his 6-foot-4, 225-pound frame to improbably recover the loose ball.

That elicited an approving chant of "Bra-dee, Bra-dee, Bra-dee," on a day in which he needed just 30 minutes to regain the rhythm and touch that disappeared in Denver.

Patriots quarterback Tom Brady celebrates his touchdown pass to Martellus Bennett during the first half. AP Photo

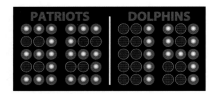

vs. Miami Dolphins, Jan. 1, 2017
Hard Rock Stadium
Miami Gardens, Florida

PATS CLINCH TOP PLAYOFF SEED

By MARK DANIELS • *Providence Journal*

MIAMI GARDENS, Fla. - The 2016 NFL season has been about retribution for this Patriots team.

First, they had to deal with being without Tom Brady for the first four games due to his Deflategate suspension. They needed both Jimmy Garoppolo and Jacoby Brissett, but went 3-1 before handing the reins back to its rightful owner.

After trading Jamie Collins, the defense was lit up by Seattle, at home, in Week 10. After that, the unit put the clamps on and finished this year allowing only 15.6 points a game to lead the NFL. Then there was Denver and the Patriots came away with a road win for the first time since 2011.

The last thing on the regular-season checklist was Miami - a place the Patriots haven't won since 2012. Last year, in the team's regular-season finale, the Patriots lost the AFC's No. 1 seed after being handed another defeat at the hands of the Dolphins.

The Patriots returned to the scene of the crime on Sunday and for the first time in four years, checked off one more box before the playoffs begin. The Patriots' 35-14 victory clinched the AFC's No. 1 seed, and home-field advantage throughout the playoffs. The Pats finish the regular season with a 14-2 record, the franchise's best record since 2010.

"I think we've proven we can deal with a lot of

Patriots tight end Martellus Bennett (88) scores a touchdown on the opening drive with Miami Dolphins safety Michael Thomas (31) defending. AP Photo

Miami Dolphins wide receiver Jarvis Landry (14) runs with the ball after a catch as Patriots outside linebacker Rob Ninkovich (50) closes in. AP Photo

things over the course of the year," Tom Brady said. "14-2 is a great place to be."

The Patriots also finished the game without any major injuries. Now, it's on to the playoffs where a bigger goal remains.

"It's awesome, man. I'm happy how the schedule came [out]," Logan Ryan said. "We got a chance to right a lot of wrongs. We just wanted to show this year's a little different and we're ready to step up to any challenge that may be presented to us."

From the start, it was clear that the Patriots would not repeat last year's dismal performance in Miami when the team lost 20-10. Last year, in Week 17, Tom Brady went 4 of 5 for 20 yards in the first half and finished with only 134 passing yards and no touchdowns. It took the quarterback one half to surpass those numbers.

On the Patriots' opening drive, Brady went 6 for 6 for 41 yards and a touchdown. In the first half, he finished with 161 passing yards and two scores. The Patriots also found more success on the ground. In last year's game, the team totaled only 70 rushing yards. They gained 100 in the first half on Sunday.

The Patriots entered the locker room at halftime up 20-7 after getting touchdowns from Martellus Bennett, Michael Floyd and two field goals from Stephen Gostkowski. Ryan also added an interception in the first half.

"Now we have to focus on what we have ahead of us," Julian Edelman said. "It's one of those things, you set goals and when you achieve those goals, in anything, just football, in life, you've got new goals to set and you go on to those ones. That's what we're on."

Miami made the game briefly competitive going on a 14-0 run to close the gap to four points. A 25-yard touchdown from Matt More to Kenny Stills brought the score to 20-14. After the brief scare, Brady and the offense took control and gained some breathing room with two touchdowns courtesy of Edelman, on a 77-yard play, and by LeGarrette Blount, his 18th of the season.

The Patriots will now enter the playoffs riding high unlike a year ago when everything fell apart in Miami and eventually the postseason.

"We talked a lot about last season and how that ended,' Brady said. "I think it's just important to keep our foot on the gas pedal."

Patriots wide receiver Michael Floyd (14) signals for a touchdown after a 14-yard reception. AP Photo

PATS' NATE SOLDER FINDS SOLACE ON FIELD

By MARK DANIELS • *Providence Journal*

FOXBORO - When he steps on the football field, Nate Solder is free for a while. Whether it be at practice or during game days, it has became his sanctuary. It's a place where his mind is focused on each play, each drive and the teammates around him.

It's a much-needed break for the Patriots' starting left tackle.

"No question. Absolutely an outlet," Solder said. "I think if you'd asked me a couple of years ago, I'd say the biggest stress in my life is football. I think now that's not the case. It's actually one of the biggest outlets and things I enjoy the most."

A lot has changed for Solder over the last couple of years. The 28-year-old became a cancer survivor during the 2014 season, when he was diagnosed with testicular cancer. He also became a father before the 2015 season. Both will change anyone's perspective on sports and life. For Solder, his outlook changed tenfold when his son, Hudson, was diagnosed with Wilms' tumor, a cancer that starts in the kidney, on Oct. 19, 2015. Hudson was three months old at the time.

Solder was on injured reserve at the time after suffering a torn biceps. Fifteen months after Hudson's diagnosis, his son is still fighting and Solder's back playing football. On Tuesday, Solder was named the team's 2016 Ed Block Courage Award winner, which recognizes players who demonstrate commitment to the principles of sportsmanship and courage.

Solder's been through a roller coaster of emotions over the past two years. As he and his teammates prepare for the AFC Championship Game on Sunday, the tackle talked about his newfound outlook on football and how grateful he is for the Patriots organization and his teammates.

"Yeah, it's been difficult," Solder said on Tuesday. "For example, Hudson's at Jimmy Fund this afternoon and he's meeting with doctors and that's kind of been throughout the season. I have to give a lot of credit to Jesus for getting me through it. A lot of times, I feel weak. Through my faith, he's carried me through a lot of it. I've got a fantastic wife and fantastic family."

After playing in four games last season, Solder started 15 games this season after missing the team's Week One game at Arizona. Since his son's diagnosis, the Patriots have rallied around Solder and his wife, Lexi. Teammates and coaches have constantly reached out. Players' wives have cooked meals for the Solder family.

On the days when Hudson has a doctor's appointment, Bill Belichick has allowed Solder to spend time with his family.

"Bill and the entire team have been really good at giving us the time we need," Solder said. "If it's

a doctor's appointment or whatever we're doing when we need to be together. So, I've been able to make almost everything. Haven't missed much of that. But there are definitely times where the thought of playing football is tough when you have so many other things weighing on your mind. I think in those moments, you remember that it's not all about us. It's not all about me and my suffering. There's a group of guys here. There's a team we represent. We move on together. Locking arms."

All teams battle through adversity. It's been that way for the Patriots this season. It'll likely they'll encounter some hardships against the Pittsburgh Steelers as well. Throughout it all, Solder's been there and will continue to protect Tom Brady's blindside.

Solder knows how lucky he is to be in this position.

"It levels the playing field for all of us because all of us are susceptible to cancer, disease, some of the tough things that so many people struggle with," Solder said. "So you realize how lucky we are just to have our health and be able to play this game and just doing the things we love doing.

"I am very thankful for all the opportunities that I have, and how close this is to all being over is just right there."

Patriots running back Dion Lewis (33) celebrates his third touchdown of the game. AP Photo

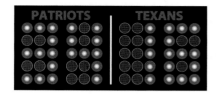

vs. Houston Texans, Jan. 14, 2017
Gillette Stadium
Foxboro, Massachusetts

NEW ENGLAND GETS JOB DONE

By RICH GARVEN • *Telegram & Gazette*

FOXBORO - The Houston Texans had three-time NFL Defensive Player of the Year J.J. Watt, and the Patriots didn't have four-time Super Bowl champion Tom Brady when the two teams met here in Week 3.

Rather, the Patriots trotted out rookie quarterback Jacoby Brissett to make his first NFL start. The advantage should have been with the Texans' defense, but it failed to rattle Brissett, because it hardly got near him in a 27-0 loss.

Compare that with the Patriots' 34-16 win over the Texans in an AFC divisional round game Saturday night at Gillette Stadium. Brady was sacked twice, hit another six times, forced off his spot on multiple other occasions, and intercepted twice while attempting 38 passes.

The Patriots obviously didn't execute, and they also clearly weren't caught off guard as the Texans' pass rush, particularly from the interior, was a point of emphasis entering the evening.

"We talked about it all week," Patriots coach Bill Belichick said before going on to praise defensive coordinator Romeo Crennel and the terrorizing twin tandem of linebacker Whitney Mercilus and defensive end Jadeveon Clowney.

"They're well coached; they have a very good coaching staff and a very good coordinator. And they're two outstanding players, everybody has trouble blocking them. They're good."

Mercilus was particularly pesky with a sack and two additional quarterback hits as he constantly got the better of center David Andrews. Same goes for Clowney, who had two quarterback hits, one coming when he absolutely rocketed through the interior line.

"They have a great front, and they're well coached," Andrews said after the Patriots advanced to their NFL record sixth straight AFC Championship Game. "They did what we thought they were going to do. There were some problems here and there. Fortunately we did enough things to win the game and move on."

If not for a 98-yard kickoff return for a touchdown by Dion Lewis in the first quarter and a 1-yard touchdown run by Lewis in the fourth that capped a two-play, 6-yard drive following an interception by cornerback Logan Ryan, the outcome might have turned out differently due to the Texans' ability to generate pocket pressure.

Lewis became the first player in NFL history to score a touchdown by rushing, receiving and on a kickoff return in a postseason game. Lewis also became the fifth player in Patriots history to score three touchdowns in a playoff game.

"He made some big plays for us," said Brady. "The kickoff return was incredible. The touchdown catch, he had a good touchdown run, so he did a great job."

The Patriots finished with 20 first downs, which matched their lowest total in the 13 games Brady has played since serving his four-game, league-imposed suspension. That was linked to their lack of success on third down as they were 5 for 14 (35.7 percent).

Patriots wide receiver Julian Edelman (11) tries to break away from Texans cornerback Kareem Jackson (25) and safety Andre Hal (29) after hauling in a reception good for 48 yards. AP Photo

Patriots running back James White (28) catches a touchdown pass in front of Houston Texans linebacker Benardrick McKinney (55) during second half action. AP Photo

Both of the Texans' sacks came on third down, and two of the Patriots' conversions came on Hail Mary-type heaves that resulted in completions of 45 yards to Chris Hogan and 48 yards to Julian Edelman.

"He (Brady) was rattled," Clowney said. "We had them right where we wanted them on third down. We were getting them in third and longs. He was throwing the ball up getting deep catches, man. He was coming up with some big plays. Take them plays away, take the kick return away, we beat them."

Which, of course, the Texans didn't do, as they lost for the eighth time in nine all-time meetings with the Patriots. But that might not be the case against the Chiefs or the Steelers if Brady finds himself in a series of similar, stressful situations.

"They tried that (interior pass rush) against us last year and had a little success, so I think we were prepared for it," Brady said. "We just didn't do a great job executing. The turnovers obviously hurt us quite a bit, so we've got to try to tighten those things up this week. Whoever we play next week is going to be a great football team, and we're going to have to play better than we played (Saturday) on offense."

Patriots cornerback Logan Ryan, right, sacks Houston Texans quarterback Brock Osweiler (17) during the first half. AP Photo

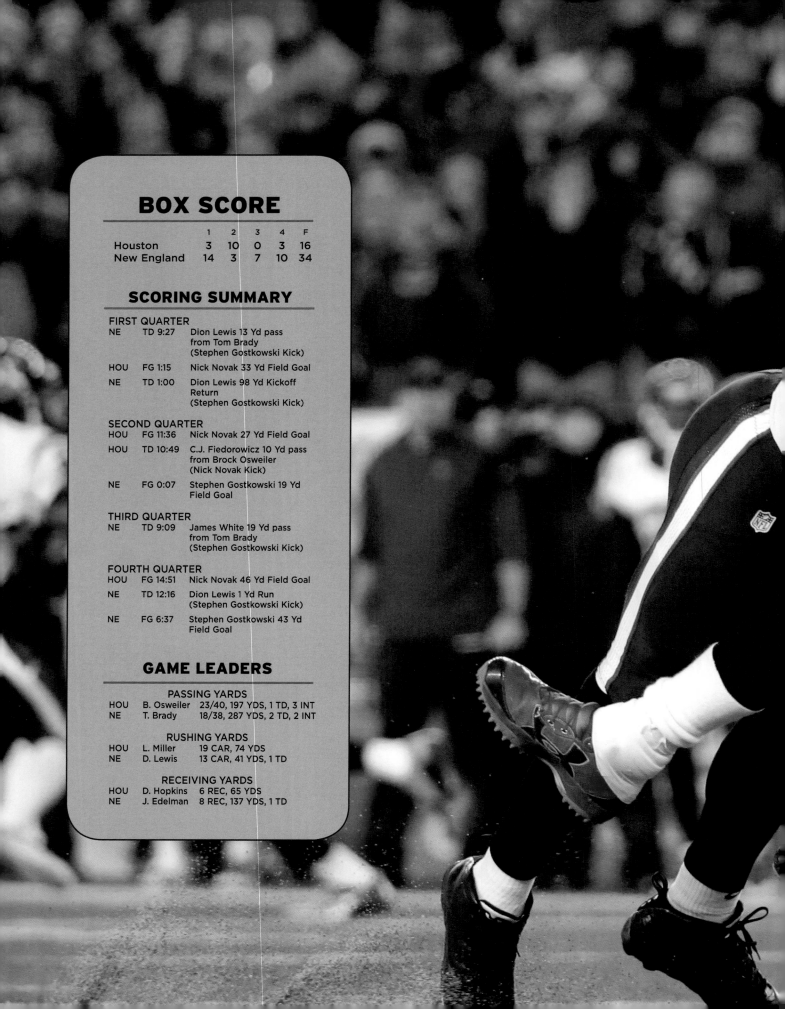

BOX SCORE

	1	2	3	4	F
Houston	3	10	0	3	16
New England	14	3	7	10	34

SCORING SUMMARY

FIRST QUARTER

NE	TD 9:27	Dion Lewis 13 Yd pass from Tom Brady (Stephen Gostkowski Kick)
HOU	FG 1:15	Nick Novak 33 Yd Field Goal
NE	TD 1:00	Dion Lewis 98 Yd Kickoff Return (Stephen Gostkowski Kick)

SECOND QUARTER

HOU	FG 11:36	Nick Novak 27 Yd Field Goal
HOU	TD 10:49	C.J. Fiedorowicz 10 Yd pass from Brock Osweiler (Nick Novak Kick)
NE	FG 0:07	Stephen Gostkowski 19 Yd Field Goal

THIRD QUARTER

NE	TD 9:09	James White 19 Yd pass from Tom Brady (Stephen Gostkowski Kick)

FOURTH QUARTER

HOU	FG 14:51	Nick Novak 46 Yd Field Goal
NE	TD 12:16	Dion Lewis 1 Yd Run (Stephen Gostkowski Kick)
NE	FG 6:37	Stephen Gostkowski 43 Yd Field Goal

GAME LEADERS

PASSING YARDS

HOU	B. Osweiler	23/40, 197 YDS, 1 TD, 3 INT
NE	T. Brady	18/38, 287 YDS, 2 TD, 2 INT

RUSHING YARDS

HOU	L. Miller	19 CAR, 74 YDS
NE	D. Lewis	13 CAR, 41 YDS, 1 TD

RECEIVING YARDS

HOU	D. Hopkins	6 REC, 65 YDS
NE	J. Edelman	8 REC, 137 YDS, 1 TD

Houston Texans defensive end Jadeveon Clowney (90) levels Patriots quarterback Tom Brady (12) as Brady releases a first half pass.

BUTLER LIVES OUT DREAM FACING OFF WITH JULIO JONES

By MARK DANIELS • *Providence Journal*

FOXBORO - Malcolm Butler stood in front of his locker surrounded by cameras. It was a good reminder of how much things have changed. It wasn't too long ago that the cornerback was an afterthought as the Patriots were heading to Super Bowl XLIX.

Now here he was, drawing one of the largest crowds a week before Super Bowl LI while wearing a personalized t-shirt that said, "Hard work pays off" with the number 21 front and center.

"You know, dreams do come true," Butler said.

That's a good way to describe the 26-year-old, but Butler wasn't talking about going to his second Super Bowl, helping the Patriots win his first Super Bowl or developing into an All-Pro cornerback. Most of Butler's dreams have come true, but in this instance the Vicksburg, Miss., native was talking about a premonition he had a little over four years ago.

While finishing up his first season at West Alabama, Butler tweeted, on Dec. 22, 2012 at 9:51 p.m., "I wanna check julio jones...lol......real talk doe."

Jones was in his second season with the Falcons and coming off a seven-catch, 71 yards performance against the Detroit Lions. This was at a point where everyone knew the NFL receiver and virtually no one knew this young cornerback from Division 2 West Alabama. But as Butler prepares for his first ever matchup with Jones and the Atlanta Falcons in Super Bowl LI, he says that tweet is a good reminder that hard work does pay off.

"That's not any trash talk or being cocky or anything. I had a vision," Butler said. "I hope young guys in college and everybody around the world can use that as an example. If you've got a vision and you work hard, you can accomplish things."

Butler heads into this championship matchup coming off his best season as a pro. This season, he set a career high in passes defenses (17) and interceptions (four). Opposing quarterbacks completed 52 percent of their passes and had a 73.6 quarterback rating when targeting the Patriots No. 1 cornerback. Butler also hasn't allowed a touchdown in the past seven games. (His last allowed touchdown was against the New York Jets on Nov. 27.)

The performance this season earned him second-team All-Pro honors for the first time in his career. Since intercepting Russell Wilson at Super Bowl XLIX, Butler has once again done the improbable - he went from Super Bowl hero and continued to get better.

As Bill Belichick mentioned on Thursday, Butler's life has changed a lot since that game-securing play in Glendale, Ari.

"It sure has - a long way from West Alabama," Belichick said. "But you know, again, and that's absolutely true for Malcolm [Butler], and I would say we have a lot of other players in that category. I mean, guys come into this league and wherever they were, this is a huge jump on a number of levels - competitively, socially, economically, the attention from the fans and the media and so forth. It's huge. Not everybody is from Alabama and Michigan and USC [University of Southern California] and those places, so for some of those guys, and even the ones that come from there, it's still a huge jump for them. It's a big part of a big time in a professional player's career - making it the first year, but then that first to second or first to second to third. That's true for everybody."

Butler became the Patriots No. 1 cornerback last season, adequately replacing Darrelle Revis in the secondary. Last weekend, he was tasked with covering Antonio Brown. The All-Pro receiver finished with seven catches for 77 yards. Butler deflected one pass as Brown caught two of three targets for 24 yards.

"I truly understand they have confidence in me and that will keep me going," Butler said of his coaching staff. "Just having confidence in me, man, that makes me feel good. Makes me go out there and play relaxed. Just to have that confidence that someone believes in me, that's all that matters."

It remains to be seen if Butler will be tasked with matching up with Jones for the entire game, but wouldn't be surprising to see the lined up opposite of each other at some point. When that happens, it'll once again reinforce how far this cornerback as come."

And once again, Butler has the stage of the Super Bowl to showcase his talents.

"Time will tell," Butler said. "It's all about performance. Talk has never won a game. You got to be about that action."

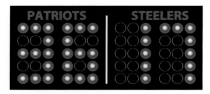

vs. Pittsburgh Steelers, Jan. 22, 2017
Gillette Stadium
Foxboro, Massachusetts

BRADY LEADS PATS TO AFC TITLE

By MARK DANIELS • *Providence Journal*

FOXBORO - The best revenge is a life well-lived.
And Tom Brady has lived his life quite well, thank you. We've seen him go from sixth-round pick to a four-time Super Bowl champion. If that wasn't enough, Brady is now one game away from achieving the ultimate revenge he has sought.

The quarterback didn't sit on his couch and pout for the first four weeks of the regular season when he was serving a suspension for his role in the Deflategate controversy. Instead, he worked. He put in extra sessions at the Dexter Southfield School in Brookline, Mass., and threw enough passes so that when his four-game sentence was over, he was able to come back with a vengeance.

On Sunday, he moved one victory away from accomplishing that as he led the Patriots to a convincing 36-17 victory over the Pittsburgh Steelers in the AFC Championship Game. Brady and the Patriots will meet the Atlanta Falcons in two weeks at Super Bowl LI in Houston.

After starting the season on a down note, Brady finds himself one win away from accomplishing his ultimate mission - a record-setting fifth championship.

"Yeah, it was a good day," Brady said. "We're

New England Patriots quarterback Tom Brady (12) celebrates after throwing a touchdown passs. The Patriots defeated the Steelers 36-17 to advance to Super Bowl LI. AP Photo

Patriots receiver Chris Hogan catches one of his two touchdowns on the day during first quarter action. AP Photo

going to the Super Bowl, man. ... Got to be happy now."

The 39-year-old set a Patriots franchise record on Sunday, throwing for a postseason career-high 384 yards to go along with three touchdowns. This marked Brady's ninth playoff game with three-plus touchdowns, tying Joe Montana for the most all-time. The quarterback is now one win away from breaking Montana's championship record of four Super Bowl wins. This will be his seventh championship game, also an NFL record.

Brady had plenty of help on Sunday. Chris Hogan had two touchdowns and set a Patriots franchise record with 180 receiving yards. Julian Edelman added 118 receiving yards and a score.

"Anytime you're on the field with No. 12 it's special," Hogan said. "You never take it for granted. He's the greatest."

After taking a 3-0 lead on their first drive of the game, Brady put the Patriots up, 10-0, by hitting a wide-open Hogan for a 16-yard touchdown at 12:13 of the first quarter.

The Steelers battled back, but after losing running back Le'Veon Bell (groin), Pittsburgh didn't have enough firepower. Backup DeAngelo Williams scored a 5-yard touchdown at 3:29 of the second quarter, but kicker Chris Boswell missed the extra point and the Pats led, 10-6.

At 7:54, Brady executed a perfect flea-flicker play. Dion Lewis took the handoff and looked ready to run, but he tossed it back to Brady, who fired it to Hogan for a 34-yard touchdown pass. Suddenly, the Pats were up, 17-6.

"He's the ultimate team player," Danny Amendola said of Brady. "He's a competitor. He's our leader and we love him. We play for Tom."

Added LeGarrette Blount: "He's the best quarterback ever."

The Steelers had no problem getting downfield on their next drive. Despite being on their own 1-yard line and a first-and-goal, the Patriots made a big defensive stand. Two runs by Williams went for a minus-4 yards. On third-and-goal, from the 5, Ben Roethlisberger's pass fell incomplete and the Steelers were forced to settle for a 23-yard Boswell field goal. The Patriots went into halftime with a 17-9 lead.

The Patriots extended their advantage to 20-9 at 10:04 in the third quarter. After the defense held the Steelers to a three-and-out to open the second half, Brady drove the Pats down the field with help from Hogan (24-yard catch). Kicker Stephen Gostkowski put the finishing touch on the drive with a 47-yard field goal.

Blount capped the next Patriots drive with 1-yard TD run to extend the team's lead to 27-9.

The defense added to the momentum on the Steelers' next two drives. First, Kyle Van Noy forced Eli Rogers to cough up the ball. Rob Ninkovich recovered to give the offense the ball at the 28-yard line. Four plays later, Brady hit Edelman for a 10-yard touchdown. Gostkowski missed the extra point and the Pats led, 33-9, at 1:40 of the third.

"This is what you fight for," Edelman said. "This is what you train for. This is what you get hurt for... to get an opportunity to play in this game."

An Eric Rowe interception, at 10:26 of the fourth, resulted in a 26-yard Gostkowski field goal and a 36-9 lead.

The Steelers scored late and the score was 36-17, but soon enough, the game was over and confetti was falling from the Foxboro sky.

"It's been really spectacular," Brady said. "We should enjoy this. Really, you never know if you'll get these opportunities in life. Fortunately, this team has got the opportunity. Now, we've got to do something and try to go take advantage of it."

Sensing the game was out of reach, fans in Gillette Stadium started chanting "Roger! Roger!" The NFL commissioner, who hasn't been to Foxboro since before Deflategate, will have a difficult time avoiding Brady and the Patriots in Houston.

The only time they would have to be face-to-face is if the Patriots win the Super Bowl. For Brady, a better ending couldn't be written.

BOX SCORE

	1	2	3	4	F
Pittsburgh	0	9	0	8	17
New England	10	7	16	3	36

SCORING SUMMARY

FIRST QUARTER
NE   FG 13:08   Stephen Gostkowski 31 Yd Field Goal

NE   TD 2:47   Chris Hogan 16 Yd pass from Tom Brady (Stephen Gostkowski Kick)

SECOND QUARTER
PIT   TD 11:31   DeAngelo Williams 5 Yd Run (Chris Boswell PAT failed)

NE   TD 7:43   Chris Hogan 34 Yd pass from Tom Brady (Stephen Gostkowski Kick)

PIT   FG 1:39   Chris Boswell 23 Yd Field Goal

THIRD QUARTER
NE   FG 9:59   Stephen Gostkowski 47 Yd Field Goal

NE   TD 2:44   LeGarrette Blount 1 Yd Run (Stephen Gostkowski Kick)

NE   TD 1:35   Julian Edelman 10 Yd pass from Tom Brady (Stephen Gostkowski failed)

FOURTH QUARTER
NE   FG 6:24   Stephen Gostkowski 26 Yd Field Goal

PIT   TD 3:36   Cobi Hamilton 30 Yd pass from Ben Roethlisberger (Ben Roethlisberger Pass to DeAngelo Williams for Two-Point Conversion)

GAME LEADERS

PASSING YARDS
PIT   B. Roethlisberger   31/47, 314 YDS, 1 TD, 1 INT

NE   T. Brady   32/42, 384 YDS, 3 TD, 0 INT

RUSHING YARDS
PIT   D. Williams   14 CAR, 34 YDS, 1 TD

NE   L. Blount   16 CAR, 47 YDS, 1 TD

RECEIVING YARDS
PIT   A. Brown   7 REC, 77 YDS

NE   C. Hogan   9 REC, 180 YDS, 2 TD

VENGEANCE TOUR COMING TO HOUSTON

By RICH GARVEN • *Telegram & Gazette Staff*

FOXBORO - The Patriots do a terrific job of blocking out the noise, in particular when it comes to any slights - be they real or perceived.

That ability to not get distracted by outside opinions or actions is a coaching cornerstone of Bill Belichick and one of the reasons his team here has been so successful for so long.

But the Patriots only block out the noise after they've listened to it, fed off it and stored it away.

That was again obvious after they dismantled and defeated the Pittsburgh Steelers, 36-17, in the AFC Championship on Sunday to deliver this once pitiful and now proud franchise its seventh trip to the Super Bowl in the past 16 seasons, a remarkable achievement in the salary-cap era.

With red and blue confetti falling on a drizzly night and his championship-gear clad players looking up, owner Robert Kraft stood on a podium on the turf at Gillette Stadium and accepted the Lamar Hunt Trophy from ex-Patriot great Tedy Bruschi.

Asked to say a few words about a team that has won 16 of 18 games and hasn't lost since Nov. 13, Kraft couldn't resist taking a veiled jab at the jealous Patriot haters from coast to coast and the marked man in New York, that being Roger Goodell, who dispensed heavy-handed justice to his BFF QB.

"For a number of reasons, all of you in this stadium understand how big this win was," Kraft said as the Fickle Foxboro Faithful roared its approval.

The No. 1 reason was the vengeful Patriots had just given Goodell the one-finger salute and, in

---

Tight end Martellus Bennett (88) celebrates the AFC Championship win by doing a little dance with the Patriots cheerleaders. AP Photo

their steely eyes, took another step toward completely vindicating themselves of those cheating charges.

Because, make no mistake, this is a team that hasn't forgotten that Tom Brady begrudgingly accepted a four-game suspension from the league for - assuming he was guilty of participating in Deflategate - what amounted to being a secondary accomplice in a petty theft crime.

The Patriots came out of that suspension 3-1 and have since gone 13-1 as the 39-year-old Brady has played some of the best football of his 17-year career. Credit Goodell for the unintended consequence of firing up Brady (even more than usual) by sitting him down.

Brady lives to be publicly doubted, so he can in turn be privately motivated. No one gets a free pass.

It's near legendary how Brady has been driven his whole career by the fact he was drafted 199th overall in 2000. But he also doesn't absolve the Patriots just because they finally took him in the sixth round as he has frequently pointed out they passed on him 198 times.

But Brady - visibly smiling on the outside, likely snickering on the inside - offered up some perfect Patriot parlance when asked after Sunday's game how personally satisfying it was to know he'd be starting in the final NFL game of a season that started with him being suspended.

"There are only two teams standing left standing, and I'm happy we're one of them," Brady politely said.

Defensive co-captain Devin McCourty at least acknowledged what everyone was thinking - that Brady and the Patriots are on a revenge mission - but also took the upbeat approach.

"I think it's a great story," McCourty said, "but I think right now our focus is got to go out to Houston in a couple of weeks and try to win it. I think that makes the story even better."

The Patriots will meet the high-flying Atlanta Falcons on Feb. 5 in Super Bowl LI in Houston. Should they win, it'll be the Lombardi Trophy that Kraft accepts. The presenter, presuming he doesn't have someplace else to be, will be Goodell.

The prospect of Goodell handing hardware to Kraft, Belichick and Brady is very real. And very motivating.

There is going to be a lot of noise coming out of Houston next week with regard to Brady and Deflategate, suspension and redemption.

The Patriots will block it out, as they always do. But only after they listen to it and feed off it, just as they have done all season in their bid to right the wrong inflicted on the best and most beloved player this franchise has ever - and will ever - have.

Patriots offensive guard Ted Karras (75), rookie offensive guard Joe Thuney (62), and fullback James Develin (46) hold up their championship jerseys as they celebrate winning the AFC Championship. AP Photo

JOSH MCDANIELS

PATS' MCDANIELS LEADS CREATIVE OFFENSIVE ATTACK

By RICH GARVEN • *Telegram & Gazette*

The Atlanta Falcons' defense is defined by across-the-board speed and front-to-back depth.

That'll be the challenge the Patriots face when they meet the NFC champions on Feb. 5 in Super Bowl LI at NRG Stadium in Houston.

"Overall they have usually nine or 10 players on the field that I would say are fast," coach Bill Belichick said. "Atlanta rolls those guys in and out of there quite a bit, [too]."

Conversely, the Falcons will be confronted by an offense that is as versatile as a five-way tool, as creative as a craft brewer and as adaptable as a hiker on the Appalachian Trial. And, oh yeah, it's a productive unit that's overseen by the smartest and savviest quarterback in the NFL.

The Patriots have the personnel to go slow or fast, heavy or light, compact or spread under crafty coordinator Josh McDaniels and the estimable Tom Brady. So no matter what an opponent sees from them on tape, they always seem to have a new wrinkle to unfold on game day.

"We've got a lot of guys that can help us be productive on offense in a lot of different ways and in different roles," McDaniels said. "You look at what you have available to you and you look at how the other team plays you, or how you think they're going to play you in those groupings, and then try to make the best decisions you can to gain the most advantage.

"That's why sometimes certain things are - maybe it's more of a fullback and two tight ends and another week maybe it's three receivers, a fullback and a tailback. There are a lot of different things that you can use. Hopefully, there's a rhyme and a reason for all of it.

"Again, I think the most important thing is you're trying to put your guys in a position to have some success doing things that they do well. The defense and their matchups, that's always a critical component of making those choices."

The Pittsburgh Steelers were subjected to two doses of the Patriots' unpredictably in their 36-17 loss in the AFC Championship Game.

The Patriots utilized a no-huddle approach 4.6 percent of the time in the 12 regular-season games Brady started this season.

However, they've trended up in the playoffs. They went no huddle for six plays (8.7 percent) in a divisional-round win over the Houston Texans and for 10 plays (13.5 percent) against the Steelers, scoring a touchdown in each game while in hurry-up mode.

"You try to evaluate the opponent as best you can and be very thorough with your preparation and your study and your research," McDaniels said. "You look at your team and where we're at and what we think we can do best, and then you kind of put it all together and try to figure out exactly what you need to do to try to win the game."

Against the Steelers, that also included using a four-receiver set.

According to ESPN, the Patriots used that formation 12 times (1 percent) in the regular season and the divisional round. They turned to it 14 times against the Steelers, including 13 of 33 plays (39.4 percent) in the first half.

"We knew we wanted to do a few things out of some different groupings that we felt like could help us move the ball, make first downs and score points," McDaniels said.

As for what surprises might be in store for the Falcons. Well, even the Patriots aren't sure yet. Although you can be sure they'll dust off or unveil something that hasn't appeared much on tape, if at all.

"Whatever it's going to be the next two weeks, I don't know," McDaniels said. "Hopefully we make some good decisions about how to utilize our guys. We've got a lot of guys that can contribute in a lot of different ways and they'll be ready to do so as we head into our preparation for Atlanta."

New England fans flocked to Houston ready to cheer on the Patriots to a Super Bowl LI win. AP Photo

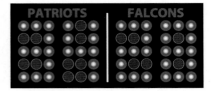

vs. Atlanta Falcons, Feb. 5, 2017
NRG Stadium
Houston, Texas

BRADY LEADS PATRIOTS TO FIFTH SUPER BOWL VICTORY

By RICH GARVEN • *Telegram & Gazette*

HOUSTON — Super Bowl tickets are expensive, a financial commitment on par with renting an oceanfront cottage in Maine for a couple of weeks or jetting overseas to Europe for a sweet stay.

But the Patriots gave fans — of both teams — their money's worth the first six times they reached the Super Bowl with the dynamic duo of coach Bill Belichick and quarterback Tom Brady.

Four of the games were decided by three points and the other two by four. The winning points were scored with 2:02 or less to play in five of the games, including with 57, 35, 4 and 0 seconds on the clock.

It was more of the same Sunday night against the Atlanta Falcons in Super Bowl LI.

The Patriots miraculously overcame many miscues and missed opportunities in the first 30 minutes to rally from 25 points down in the second half and tie the score at 28-all with 57 seconds to play.

That ensured — in typical fashion — the outcome remained excitedly in doubt to the very end, and then some, as this became the first Super Bowl to go to overtime.

Running back James White scores the winning touchdown in overtime between Atlanta defenders Jalen Collins (23), left, and Robert Alford (32). AP Photo

Quarterback Tom Brady (12) attempts to tackle Falcons cornerback Robert Alford (32) after Alford intercepted his pass. Alford returned the interception 82-yards for a touchdown. AP Photo

Then the Patriots completed the greatest comeback in Super Bowl history, posting a 34-28 victory when James White scored on a 2-yard run on the opening possession of OT to deliver the franchise it's fifth Lombardi Trophy before a heavily partisan crowd of 70,807 at NRG Stadium.

"We all brought each other back," Brady said. "We never felt out of it. It was a tough battle."

Brady, who extended his league record for most Super Bowl starts by a quarterback to seven, overtook boyhood idol Joe Montana and Terry Bradshaw and become the first passer with five rings. Brady was named MVP for a record fourth time, breaking a tie with Montana.

"I don't think there will ever be anyone else who is able to do that," Edelman said of Brady's still expanding trophy collection.

Brady wouldn't commit to whether this was the best Super Bowl win — and by extension the best of the

Julian Edelman is upended by Falcons cornerback Philip Wheeler, bottom, during first half action. AP Photo

208, and counting, victories — in his Canton-bound career.

"They're all great," Brady said when asked if this was the best Super Bowl win of his career. "This team resembled a lot of teams from the past. They have a lot of mental toughness, great defense. Everyone rose to the occasion in the second half and overtime."

Losing wasn't a topic that came up once in the past two weeks anywhere outside of Atlanta as the Patriots, despite only being tagged as a three-point favorite by Vegas, were considered virtual locks to find

Atlanta wide receiver Julio Jones (11) goes up high over Patriots cornerback Eric Rowe (25) to make the catch. AP Photo

Patriots receiver Danny Amendola (80) scores on a crucial two-point conversion to tie the game with :57 seconds remaining. AP Photo

Dont'a Hightower knocks the ball away from Atlanta quarterback Matt Ryan (2) during a huge second half play. The ensuing fumble was recovered by Patriots defensive lineman Alan Branch. AP Photo

Patriots receiver Julian Edelman hangs on to make a circus catch as the Falcons Ricardo Allen and Keanu Neal defend. AP Photo

Quarterback Tom Brady celebrates after watching James White score the game-winning touchdown in overtime. AP Photocheerleaders. AP Photo

themselves accepting the Lombardi Trophy from callous commissioner Roger Goodell.

It took everything Brady had - with a huge helping hand from White, who made a Super Bowl-record 14 receptions and scored 20 points - to ensure that occurred, providing a stupendous ending to a season that started with him serving a four-game suspension for Deflategate.

Goodell was greeted by a chorus of boos that rocked the stadium as he handed the Lombardi Trophy to owner Robert Kraft. It then went to Belichick and a smiling Brady, who held the hardware high and shouted, "Let's go."

Brady was battered and bruised, but not beaten despite being sacked five times and throwing what appeared to be a game-altering interception in the second quarter.

He finished 43 of 63 for 466 yards and two touchdowns, setting Super Bowl records for most attempts, completions and yards in a game.

Brady held the old mark of 37 completions, set against the Seattle Seahawks in Super Bowl XLIX. He surpassed Jim Kelly's mark of 58 pass attempts in Super Bowl XXVI and Kurt Warner's 414 passing yards in Super Bowl XXXIV.

"He just proved to you guys that he is the greatest, period," safety Patrick Chung said. "So all of you haters need to shut up and just own up that he is the greatest of all time. We all saw that today."

Brady was simply stupendous in the fourth quarter and overtime, which ended when White scored his third touchdown of the game. He was 21 of 27 for 246 yards and a TD to close out the comeback.

"He's the leader, the general, the best ever, and that is the end of the story," receiver Danny Amendola said.

And, as has been the story in all seven Super Bowls that Brady and Belichick have been a part of with the Patriots, it came down to the end and every football fan got their money's worth here Sunday night.

Facing page top: Coach Belichick congratulates James White on his performance. AP Photo

Facing page bottom: New England players catch up on the latest headlines. AP Photo

BOX SCORE

	1	2	3	4	OT	F
New England	0	3	6	19	6	34
Atlanta	0	21	7	0	0	28

SCORING SUMMARY

SECOND QUARTER
ATL	TD	12:15	Devonta Freeman 5 Yd Run (Matt Bryant Kick)
ATL	TD	8:48	Austin Hooper 19 Yd pass from Matt Ryan (Matt Bryant Kick)
ATL	TD	2:21	Robert Alford 82 Yd Interception Return (Matt Bryant Kick)
NE	FG	0:02	Stephen Gostkowski 41 Yd Field Goal

THIRD QUARTER
ATL	TD	8:31	Tevin Coleman 6 Yd pass from Matt Ryan (Matt Bryant Kick)
NE	TD	2:06	James White 5 Yd pass from Tom Brady (Stephen Gostkowski PAT failed)

FOURTH QUARTER
NE	FG	9:44	Stephen Gostkowski 33 Yd Field Goal
NE	TD	5:56	Danny Amendola 6 Yd pass from Tom Brady (James White Run for Two-Point Conversion)
NE	TD	0:57	James White 1 Yd Run (Tom Brady Pass to Danny Amendola for Two-Point Conversion)

OVERTIME
NE	TD	11:02	James White 2 Yd Run

GAME LEADERS

PASSING YARDS
NE	T. Brady	43/62, 466 YDS, 2 TD, 1 INT
ATL	M. Ryan	17/23, 284 YDS, 2 TD, 0 INT

RUSHING YARDS
NE	L. Blount	11 CAR, 31 YDS
ATL	D. Freeman	11 CAR, 75 YDS, 1 TD

RECEIVING YARDS
NE	J. White	14 REC, 100 YDS, 1 TD
ATL	J. Jones	4 REC, 87 YDS

After suspending him four games due to the Deflategate investigation, Commissioner Roger Goodell congratulates Tom Brady on the Super Bowl LI victory. AP Photo